Gael Art Gallery

Welcome to Gael Art Gallery in book form, size 8.5x11. GAEL is short for Joel Wayne Arconado Ganibe. The purpose of this art book is to maximize exposure for his art work. (All images copyrighted to the artist. All rights reserved.).

Please contact his face book account under his name in case you are interested to order his works or commission him to paint for you,

More of his works can be viewed here: www.facebook.com/GalleryGanibe. Joel dedicates his art to social causes. Sales from his paintings support his work as an international development consultant, specializing in education for developing countries.

Copies of this book are available online and via publisher at www.jobelizes.webs.com. Due to Gael's many paintings, hopefully further sequels of this book will be made. You can frame any of the paintings featured on these pages and hang them in walls, and still keep your collection intact by buying extra copies of this book, which is very affordable.

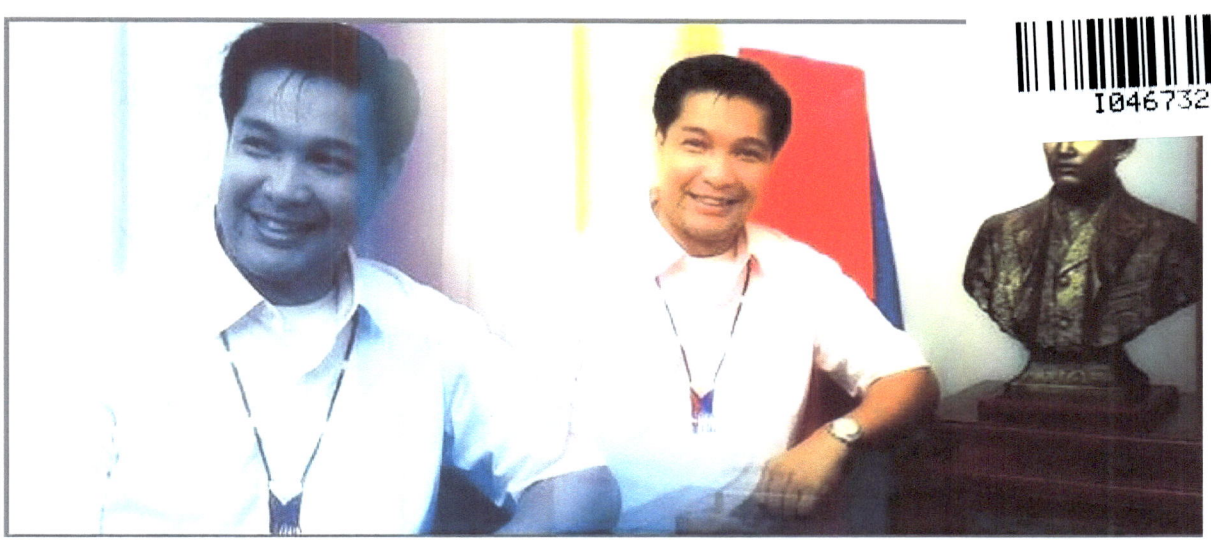

I0467323

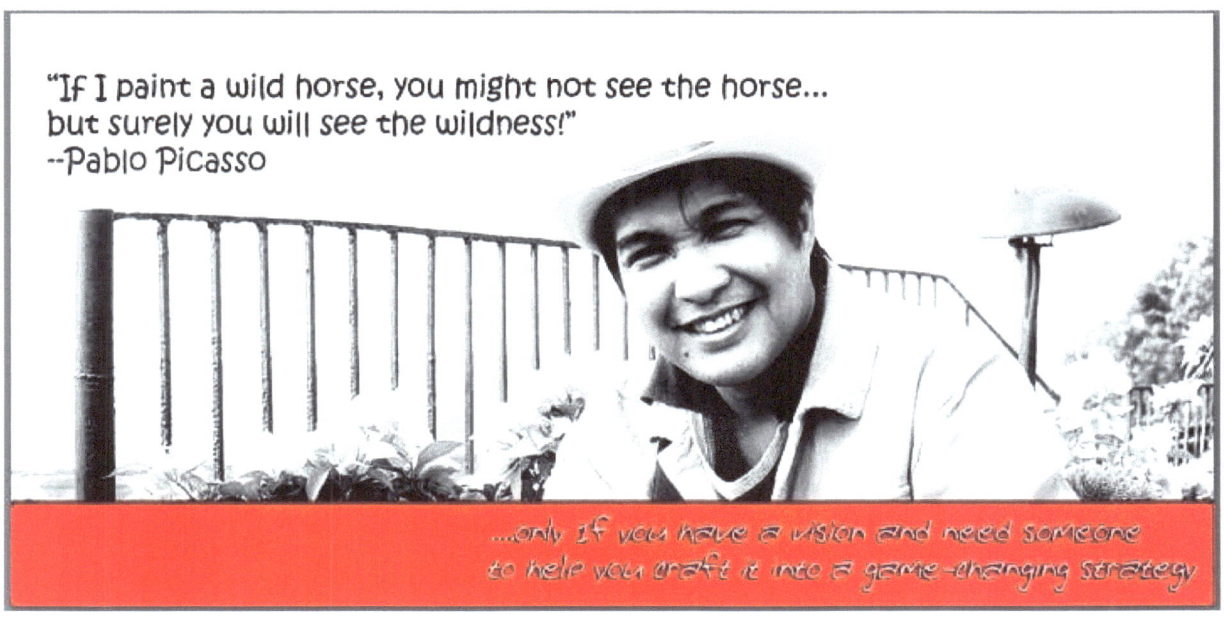

"If I paint a wild horse, you might not see the horse... but surely you will see the wildness!"
--Pablo Picasso

...only if you have a vision and need someone to help you craft it into a game-changing strategy

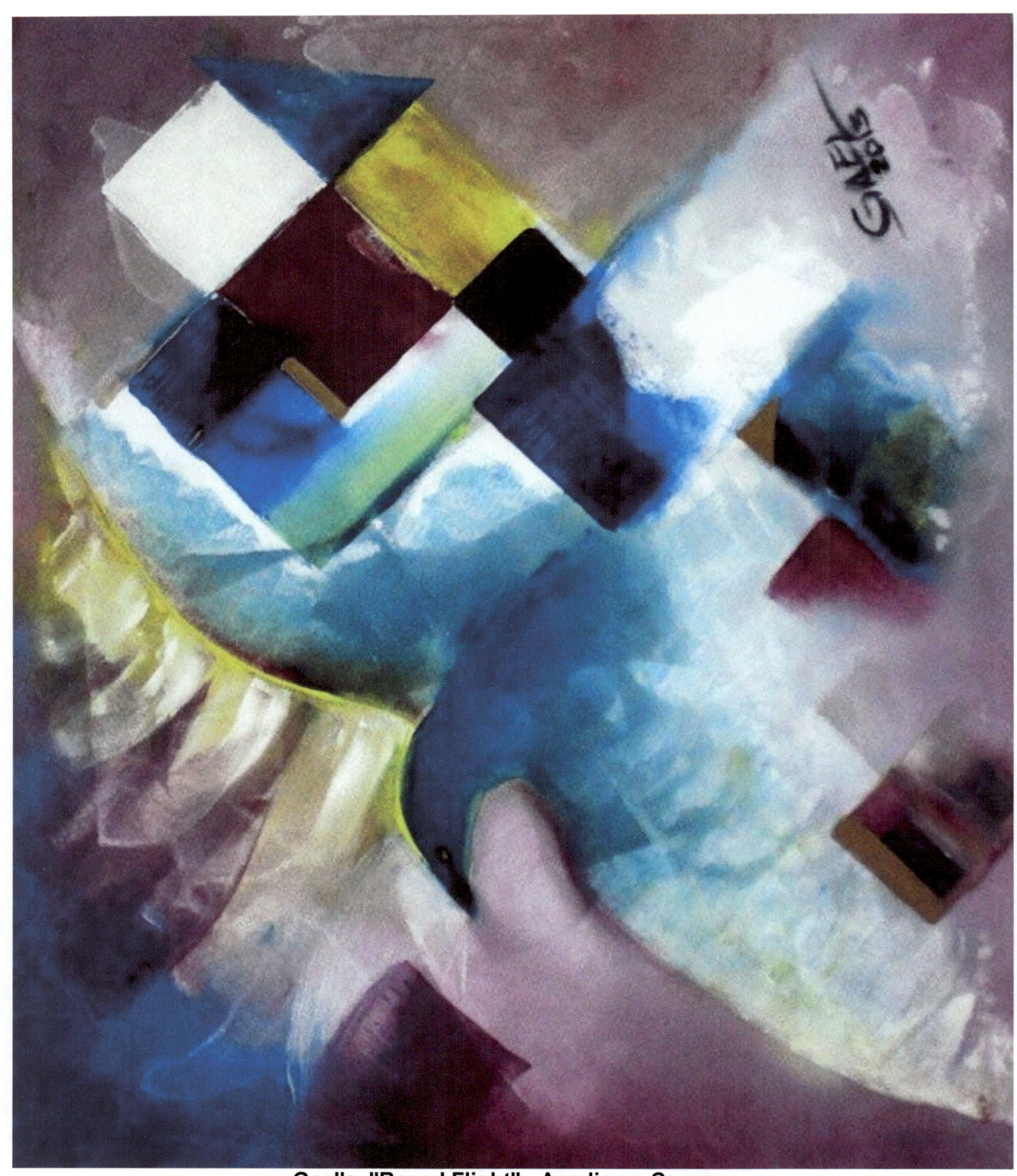

Gael's "Boxed Flight" - Acrylic on Canvas

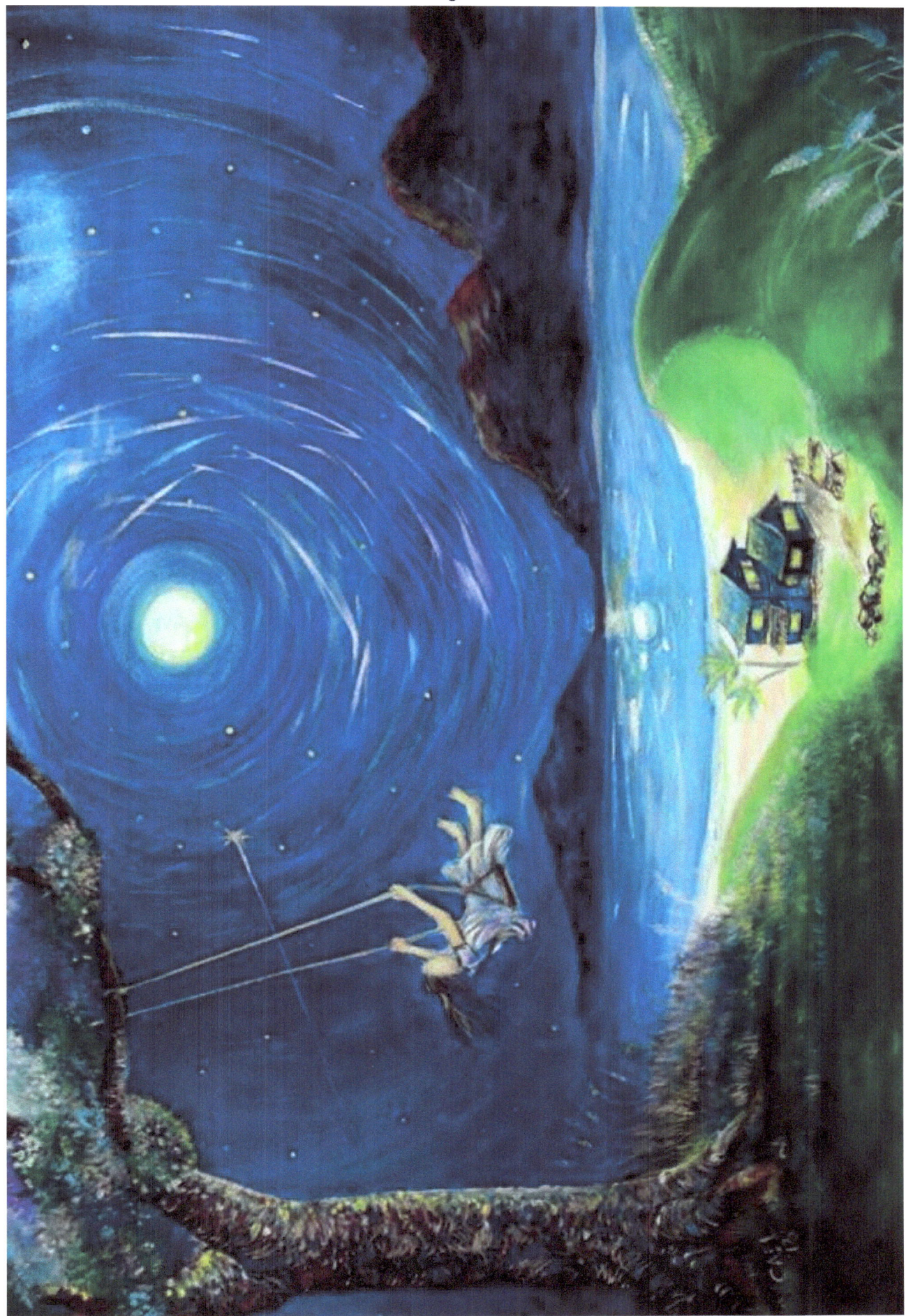

Gael's "Night Swing" - Acrylic on Canvas

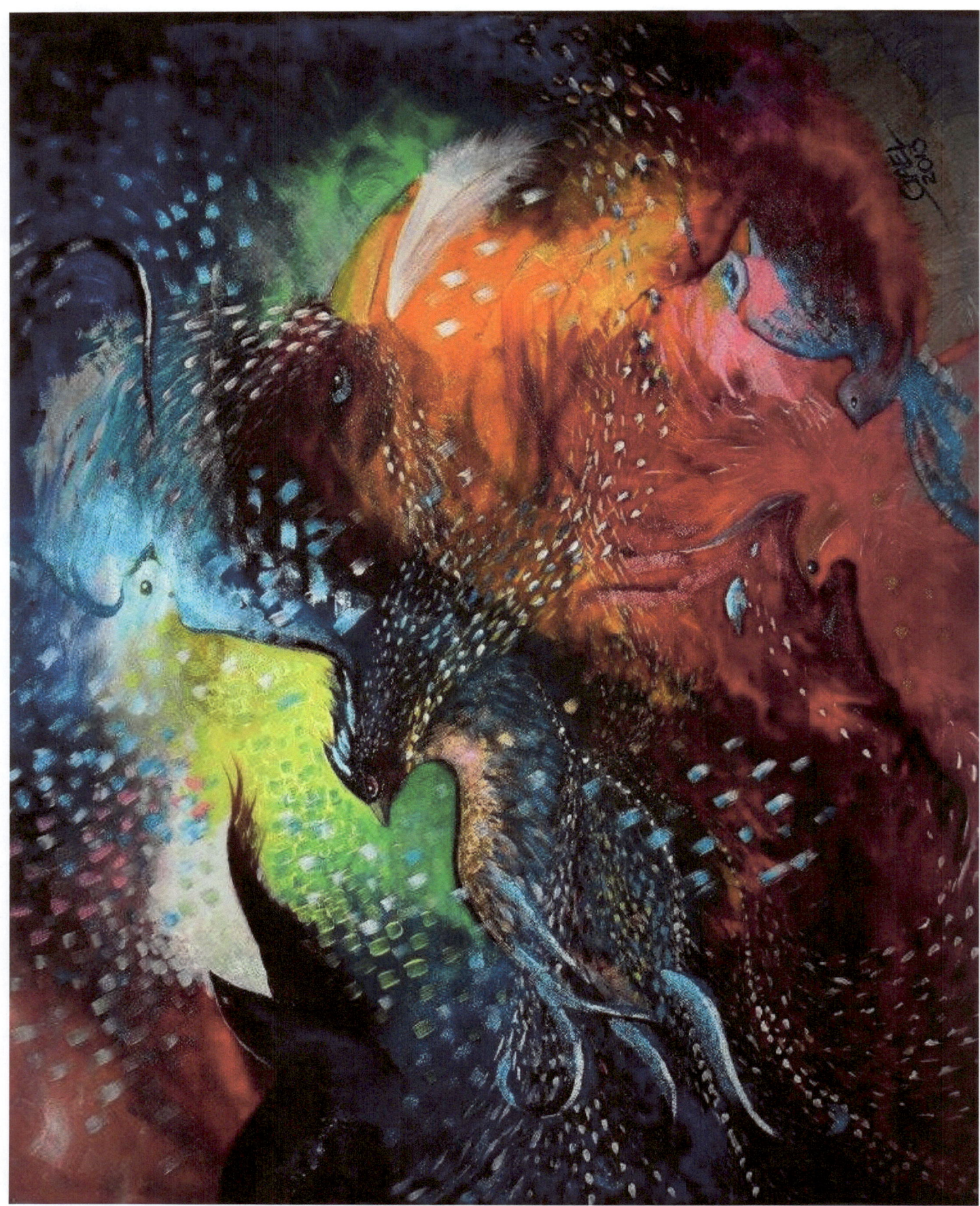

Gael's "7 Birds/Night Flight" - Acrylic on Canvas

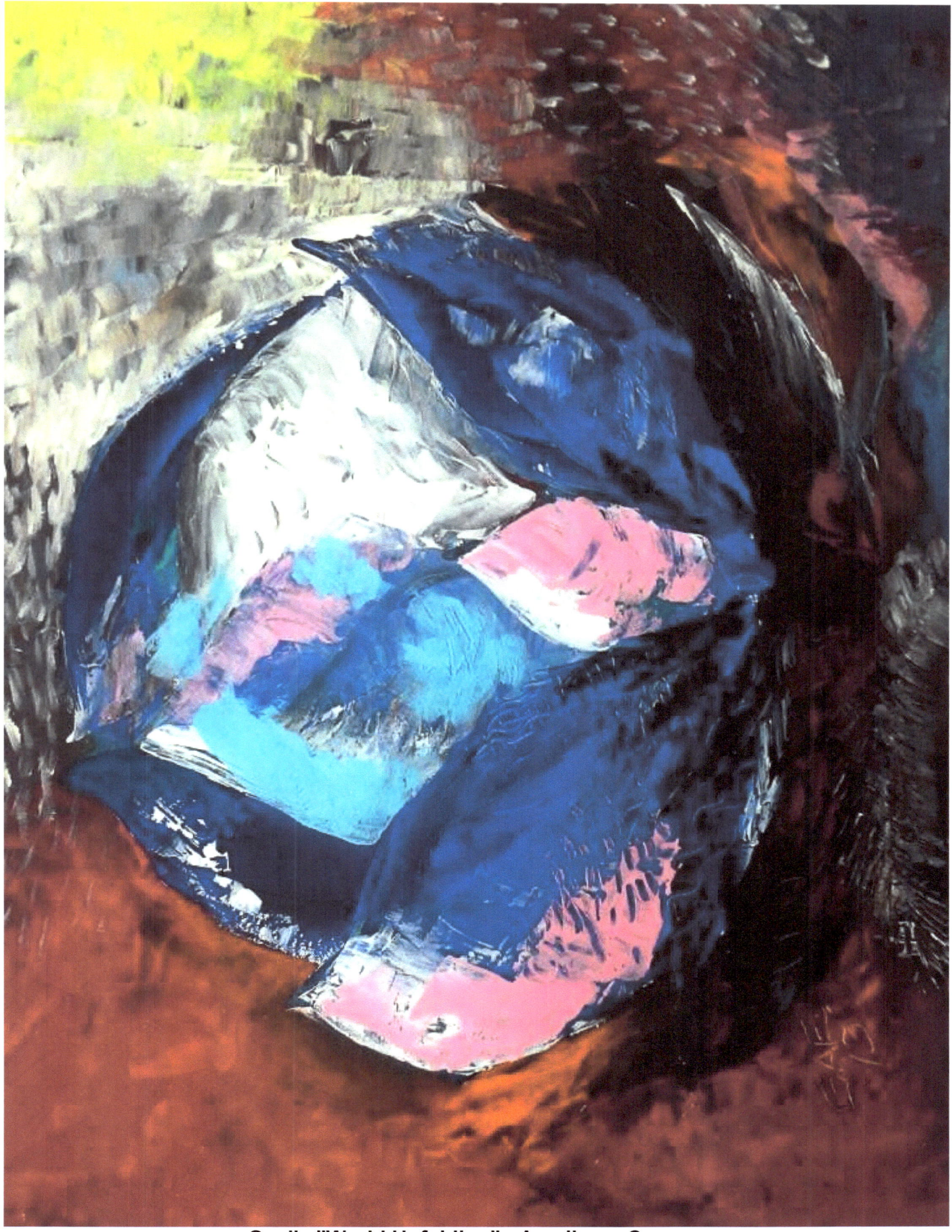

Gael's "World Unfolding" - Acrylic on Canvas

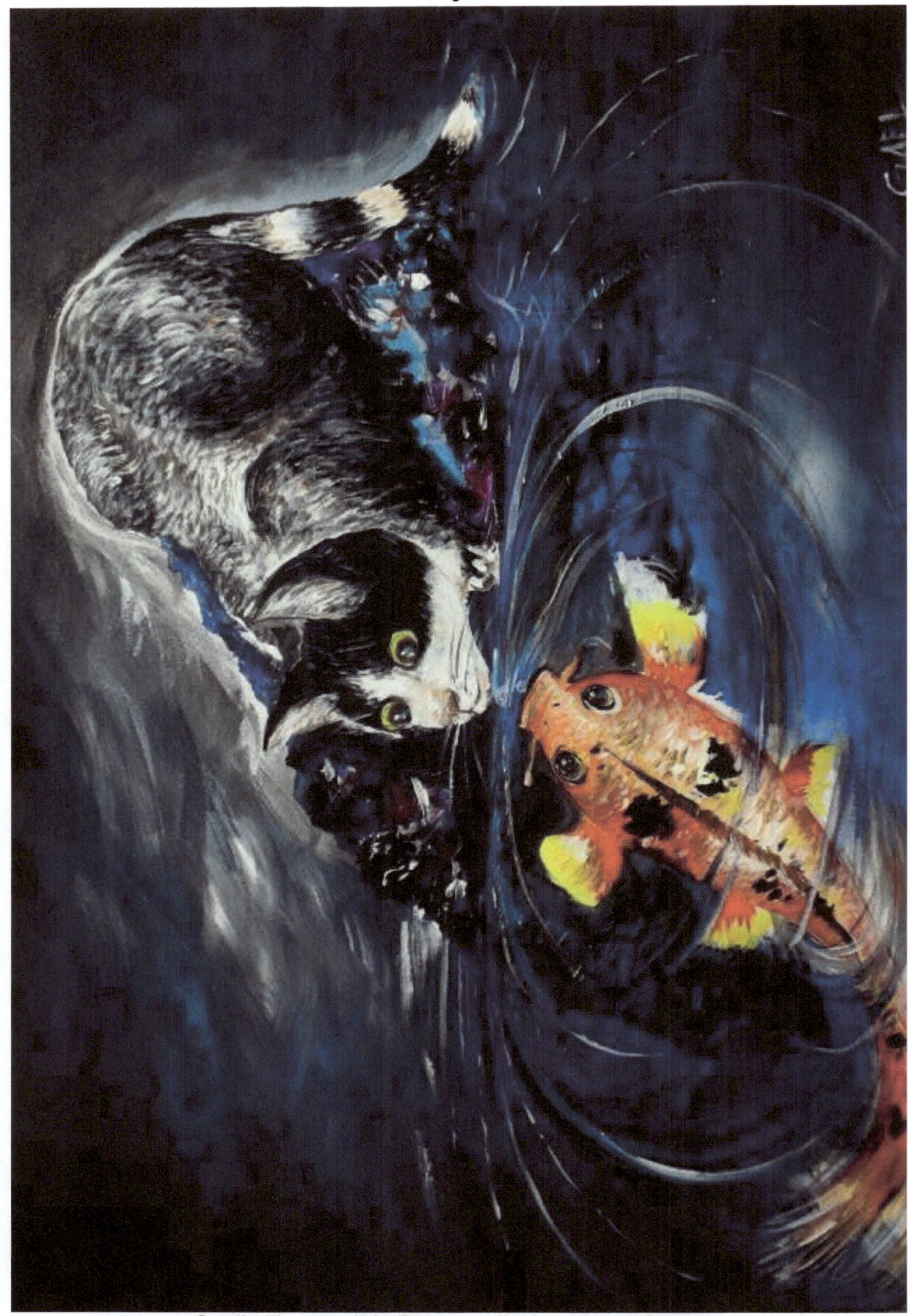

Gael's "Impossible Romance" - Acrylic on Canvas

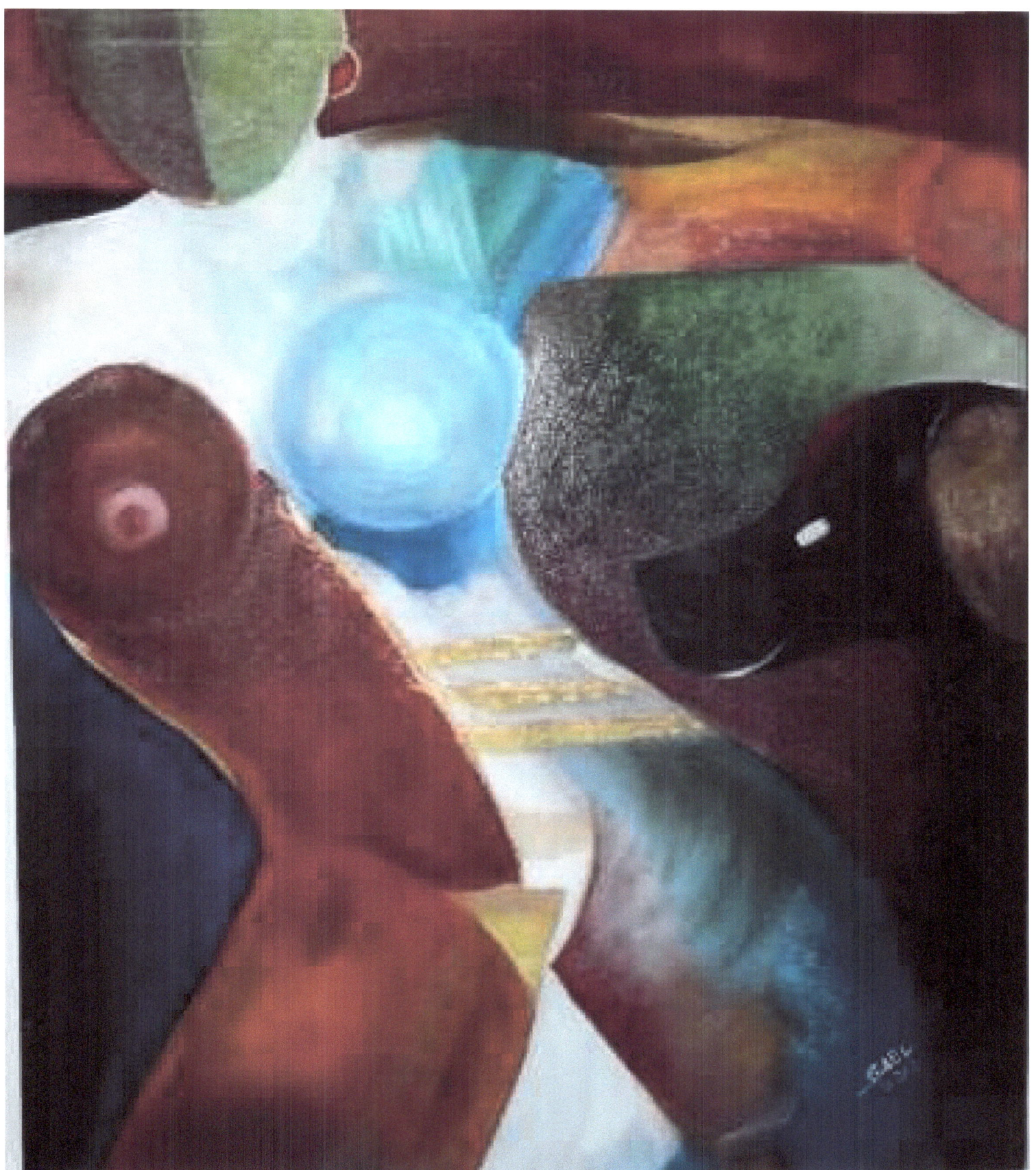

Gale's "7" - Mixed Media

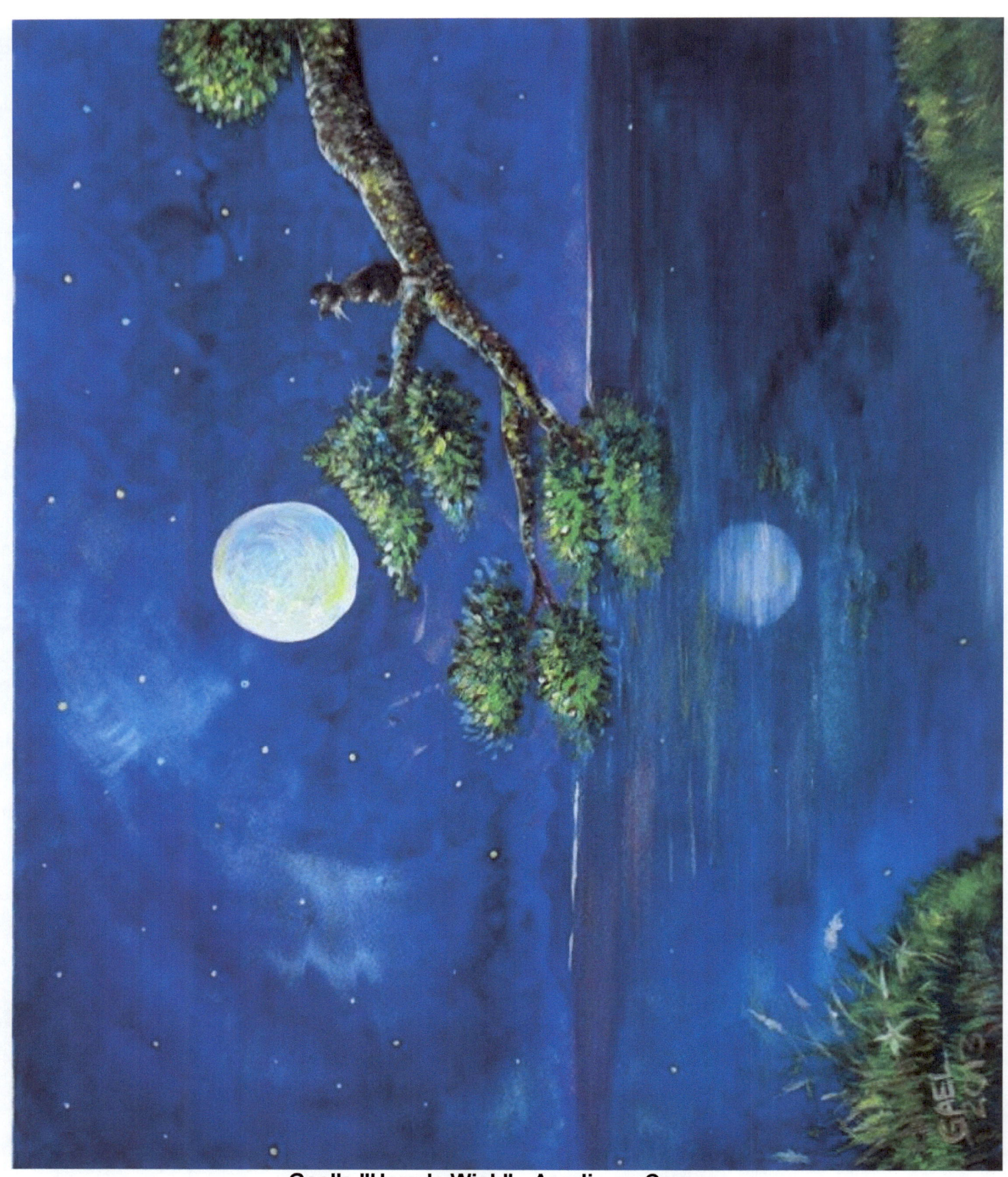

Gael's "Harry's Wish" - Acrylic on Canvas

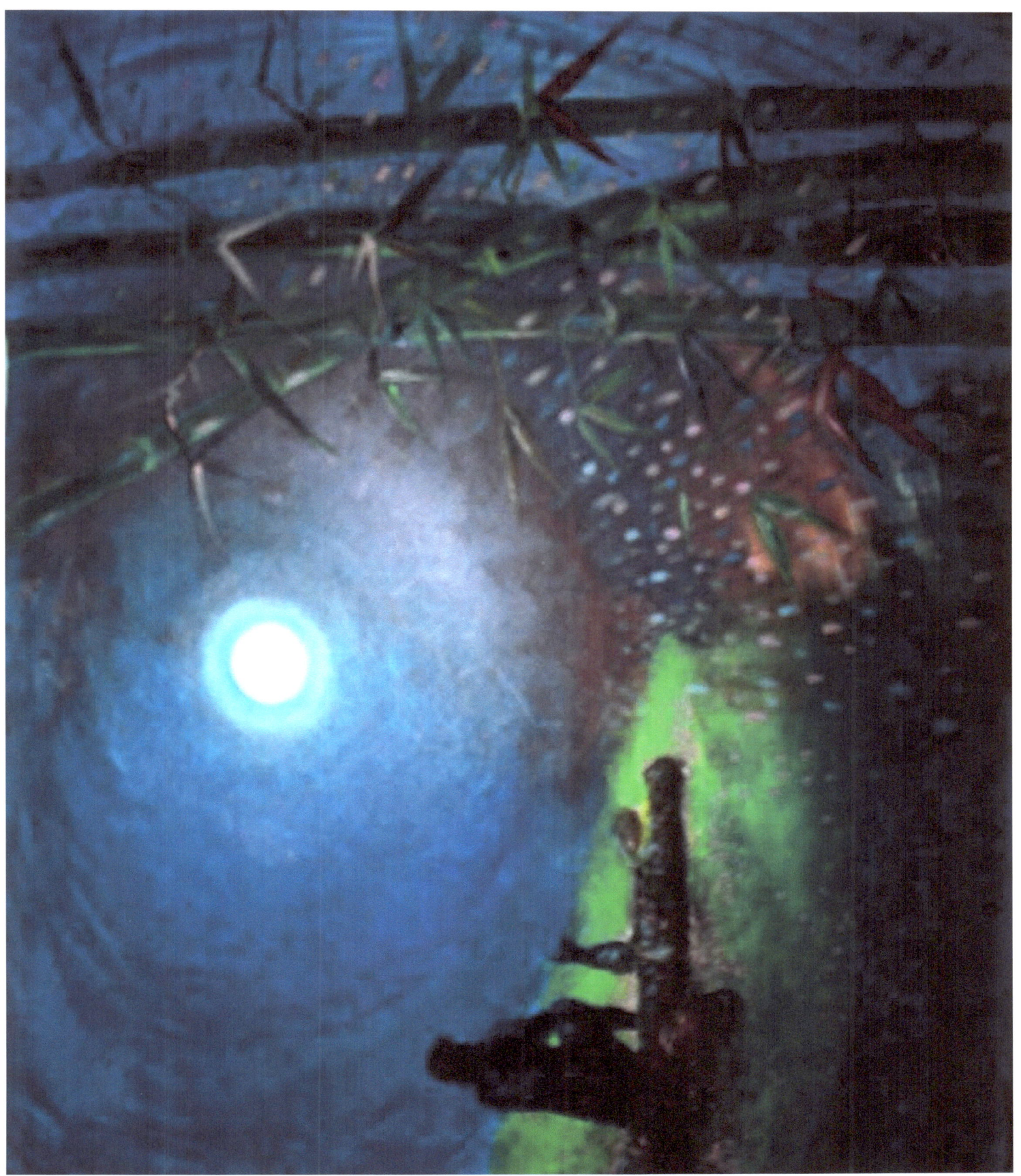

Gael's "Harry and Me" - Acrylic on Canvas

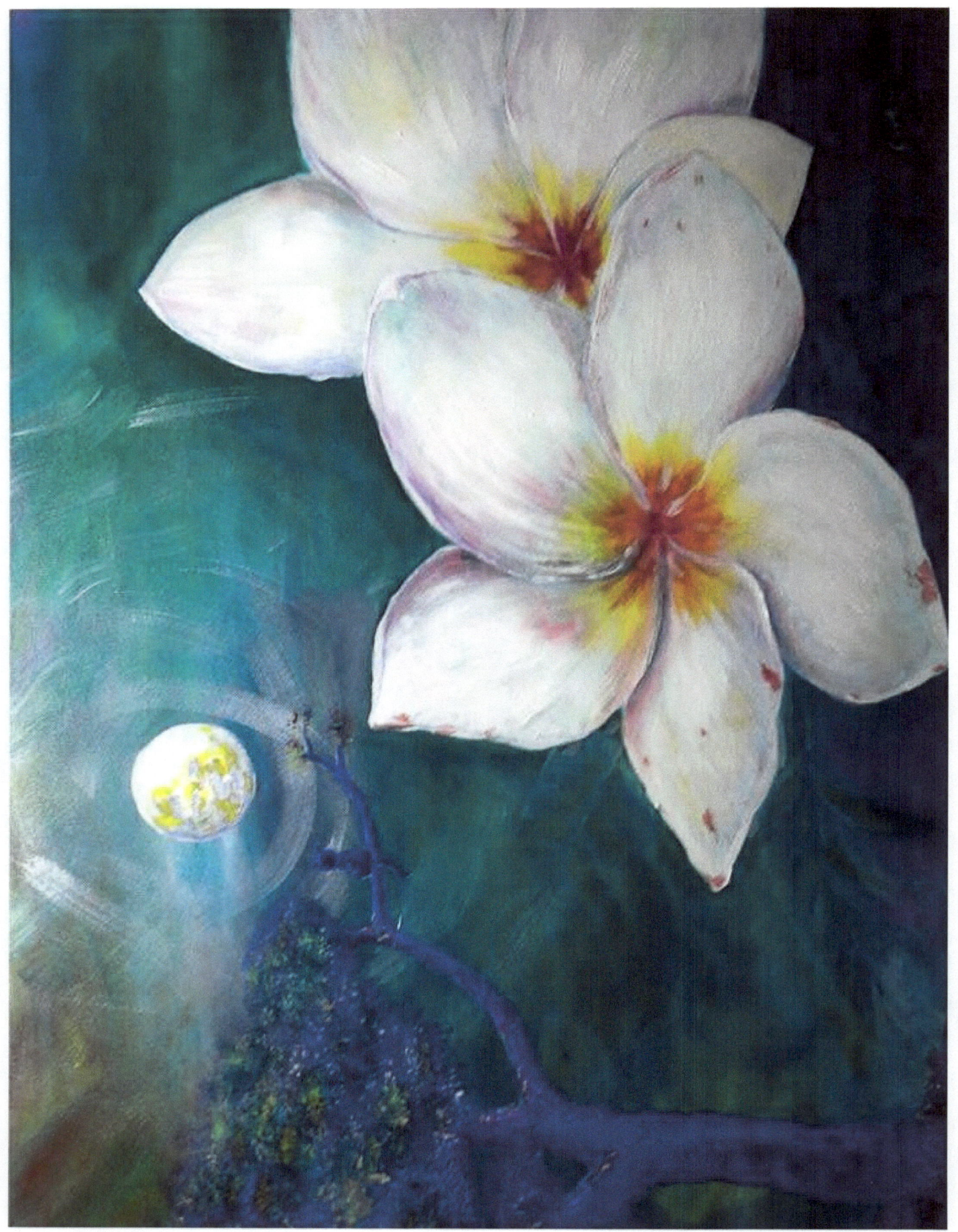

Gael's Harry's Song" - Acrylic on Canvas

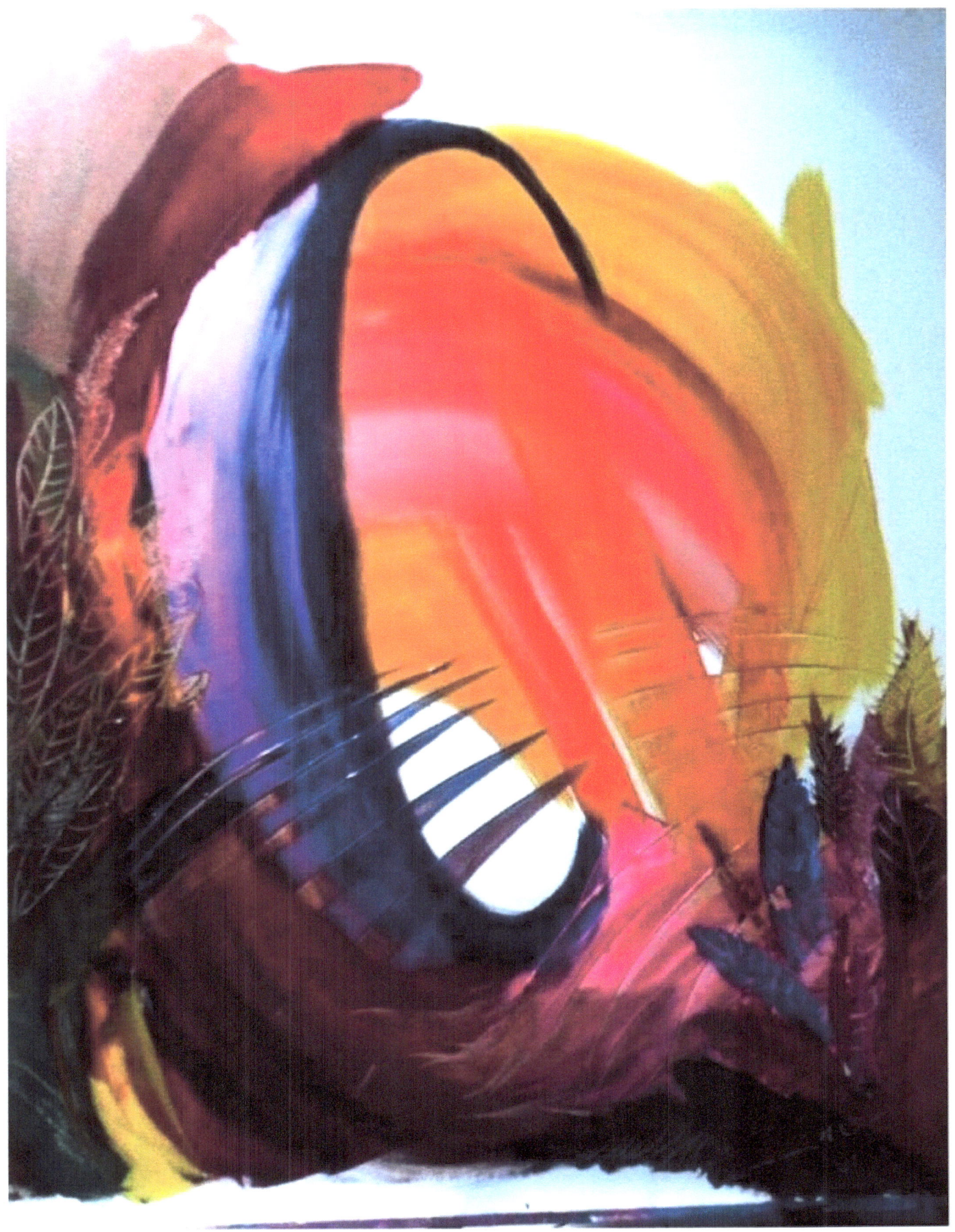

Gael's "Fresh Beginnings" - Acrylic on Canvas

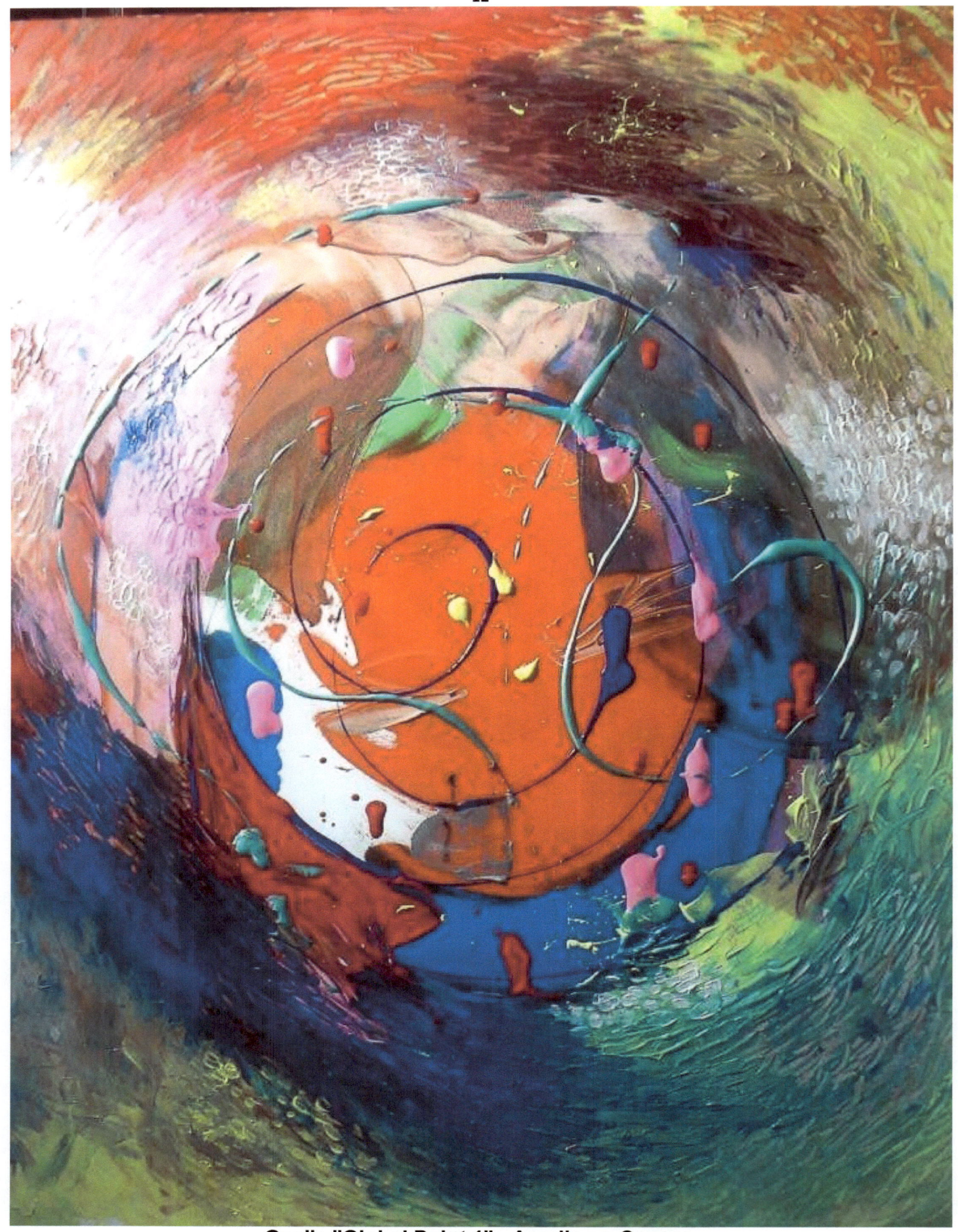

Gael's "Global Point 1" - Acrylic on Canvas

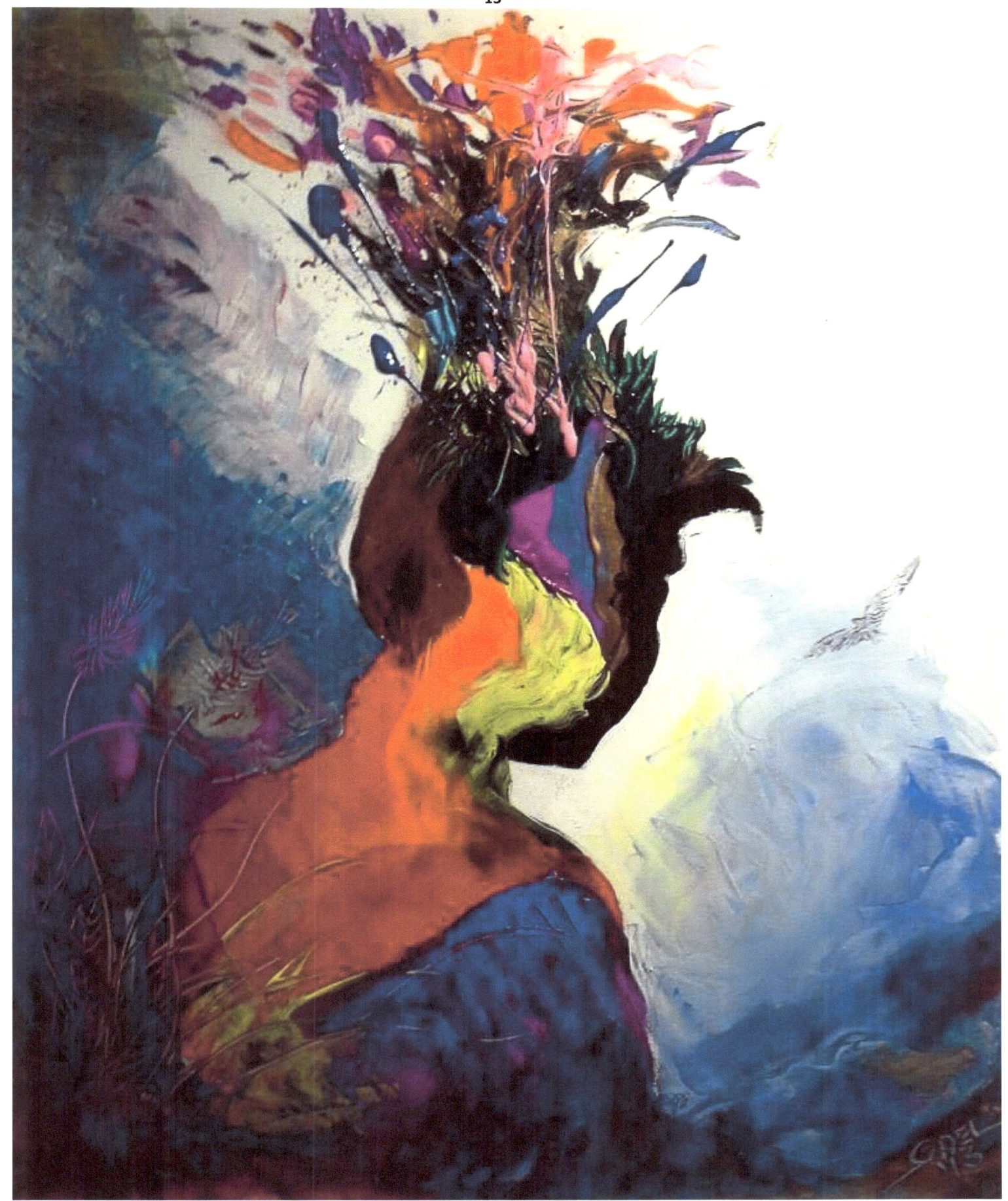

Gael's "Sabog Diwa" - Acrylic on Canvas

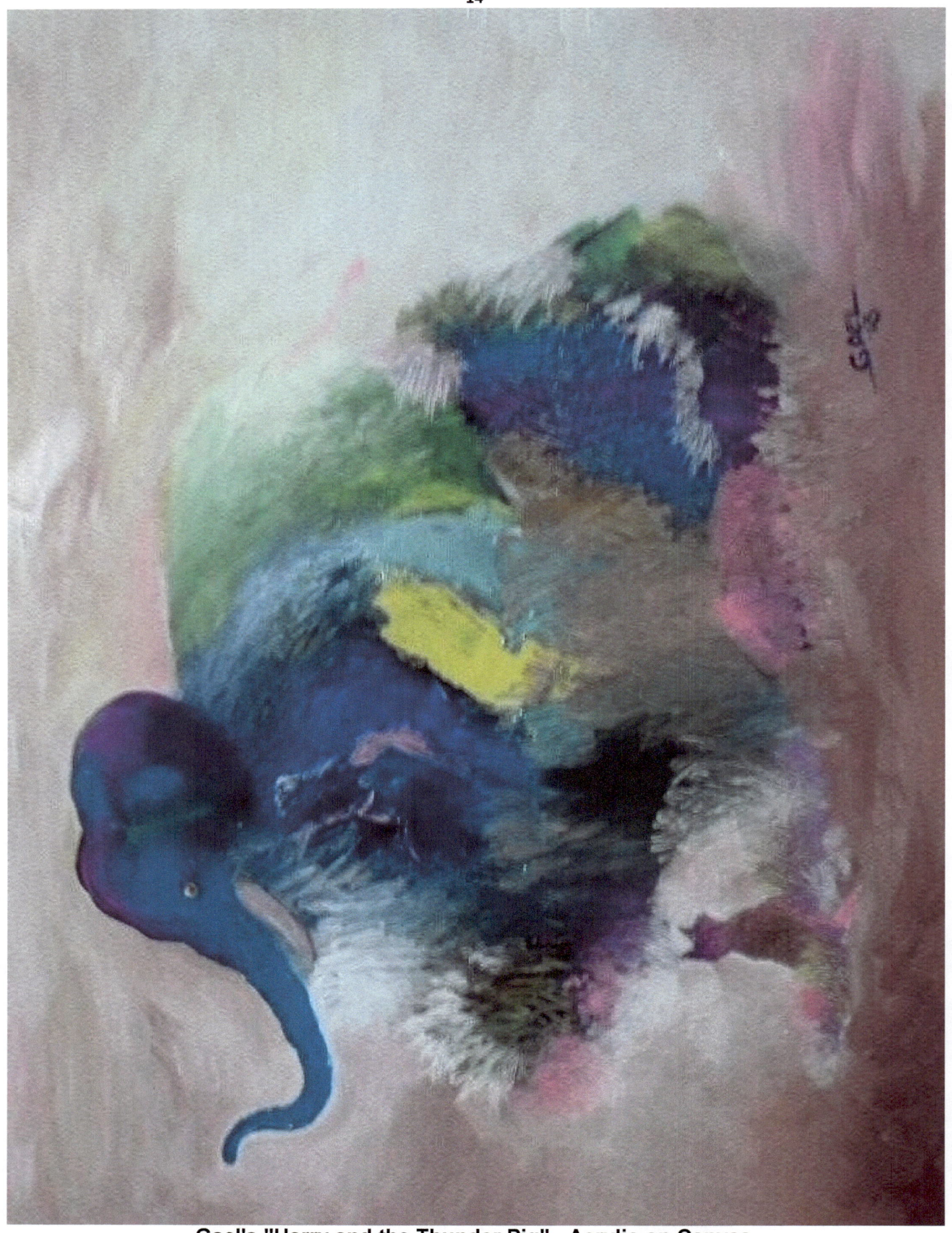

Gael's "Harry and the Thunder Pig" - Acrylic on Canvas

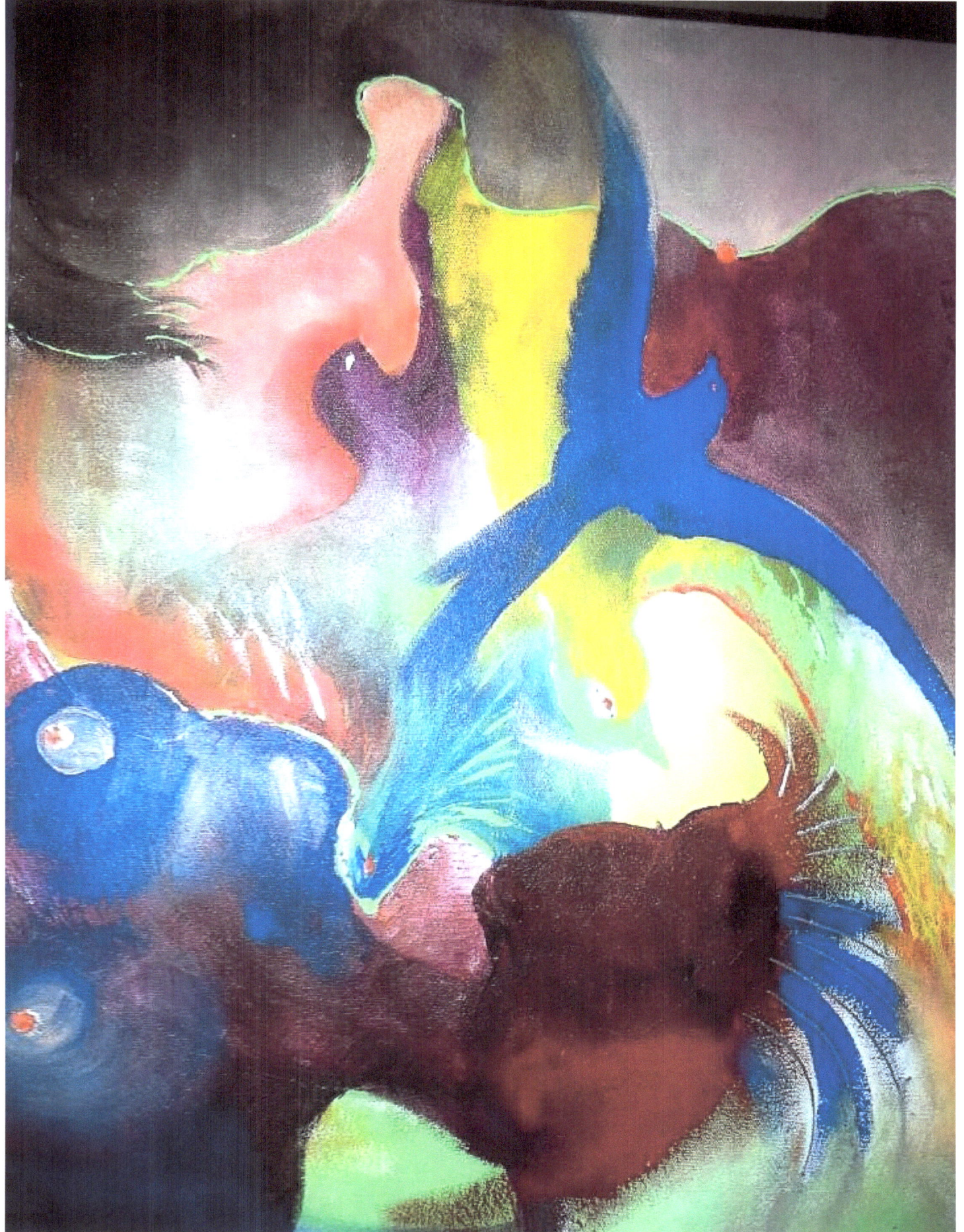

Gael's "Reversible" - Acrylic on Canvas

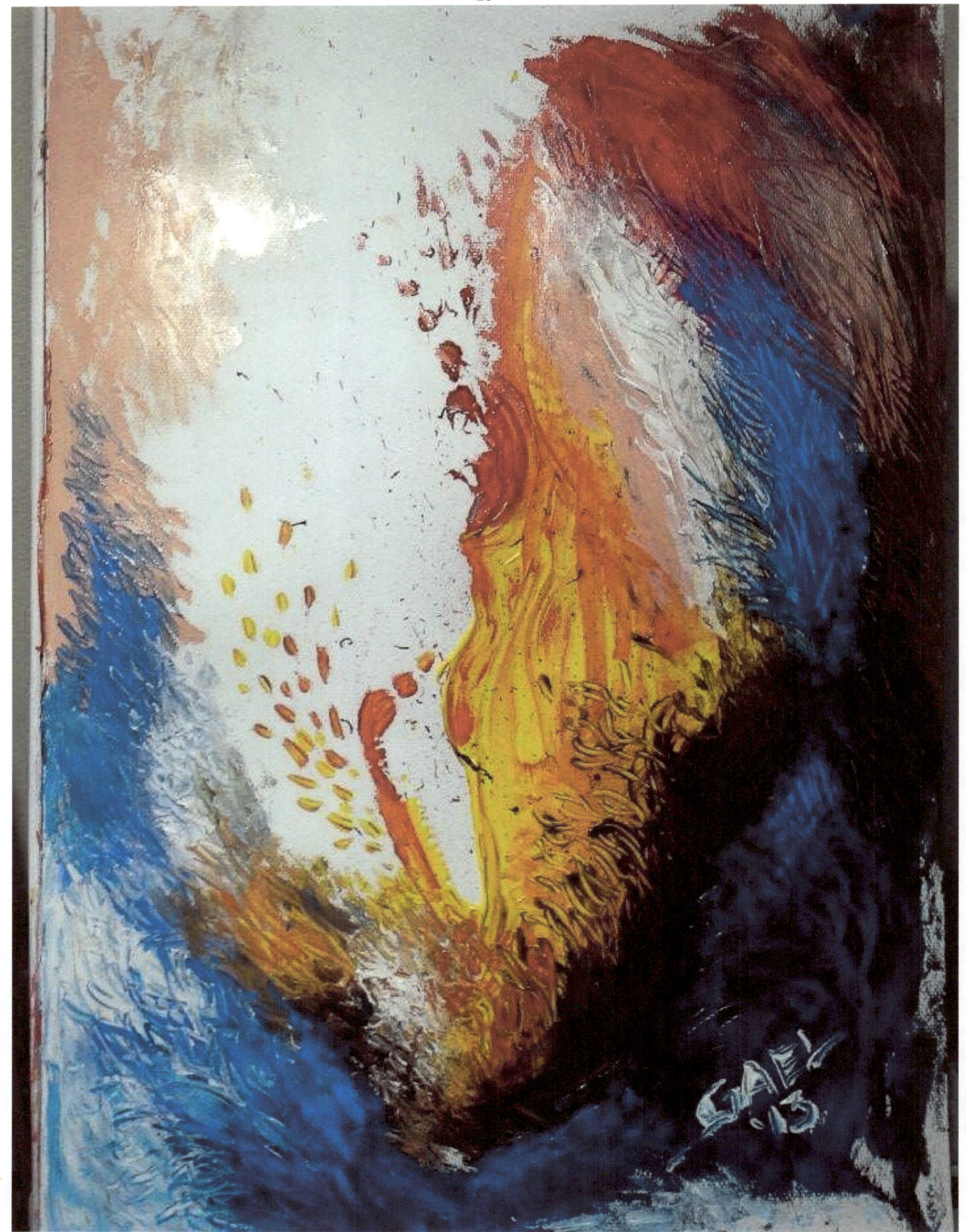

Gael's "Release" - Acrylic on Paper

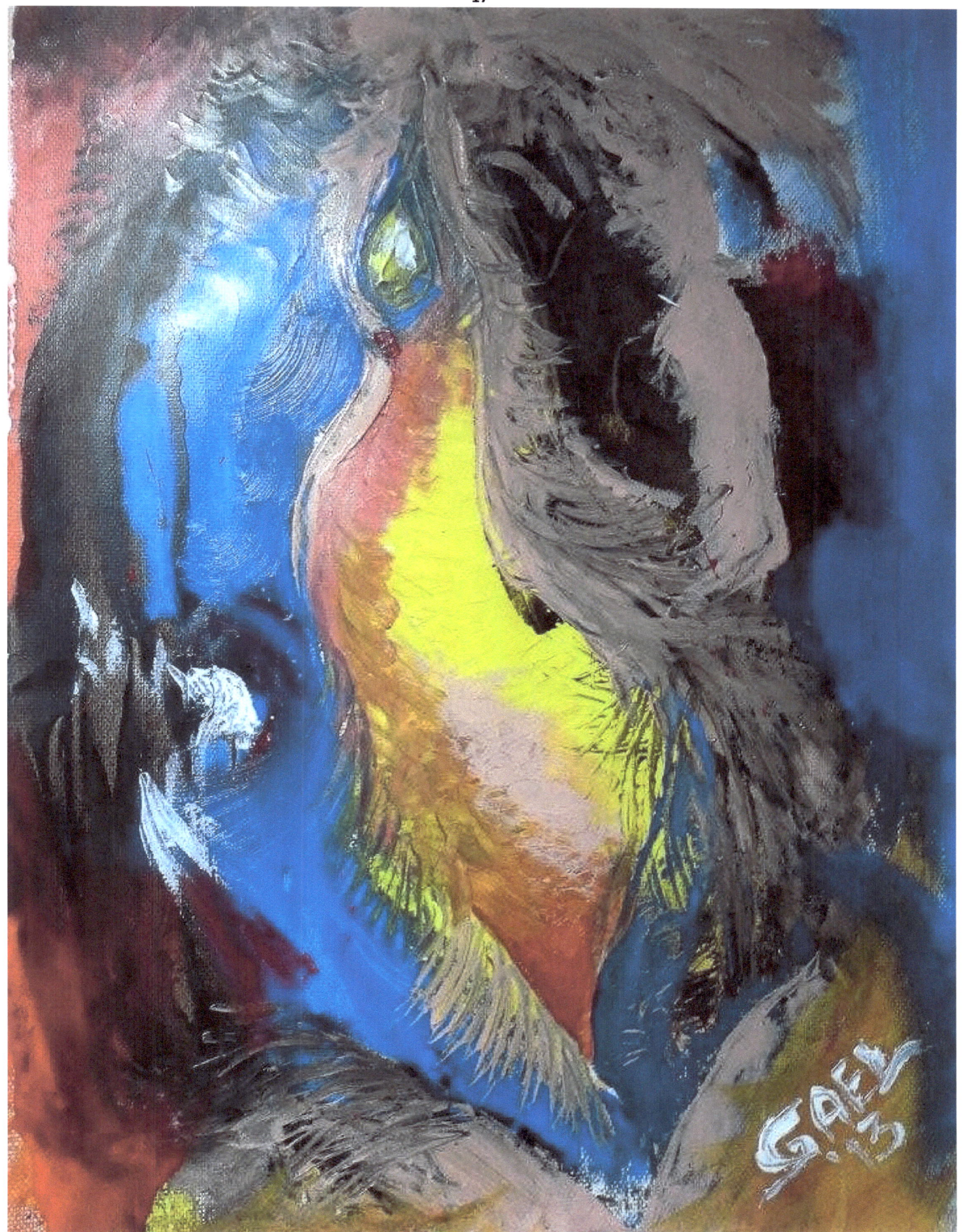

Gael's "The Singer" - Acrylic on Canvas

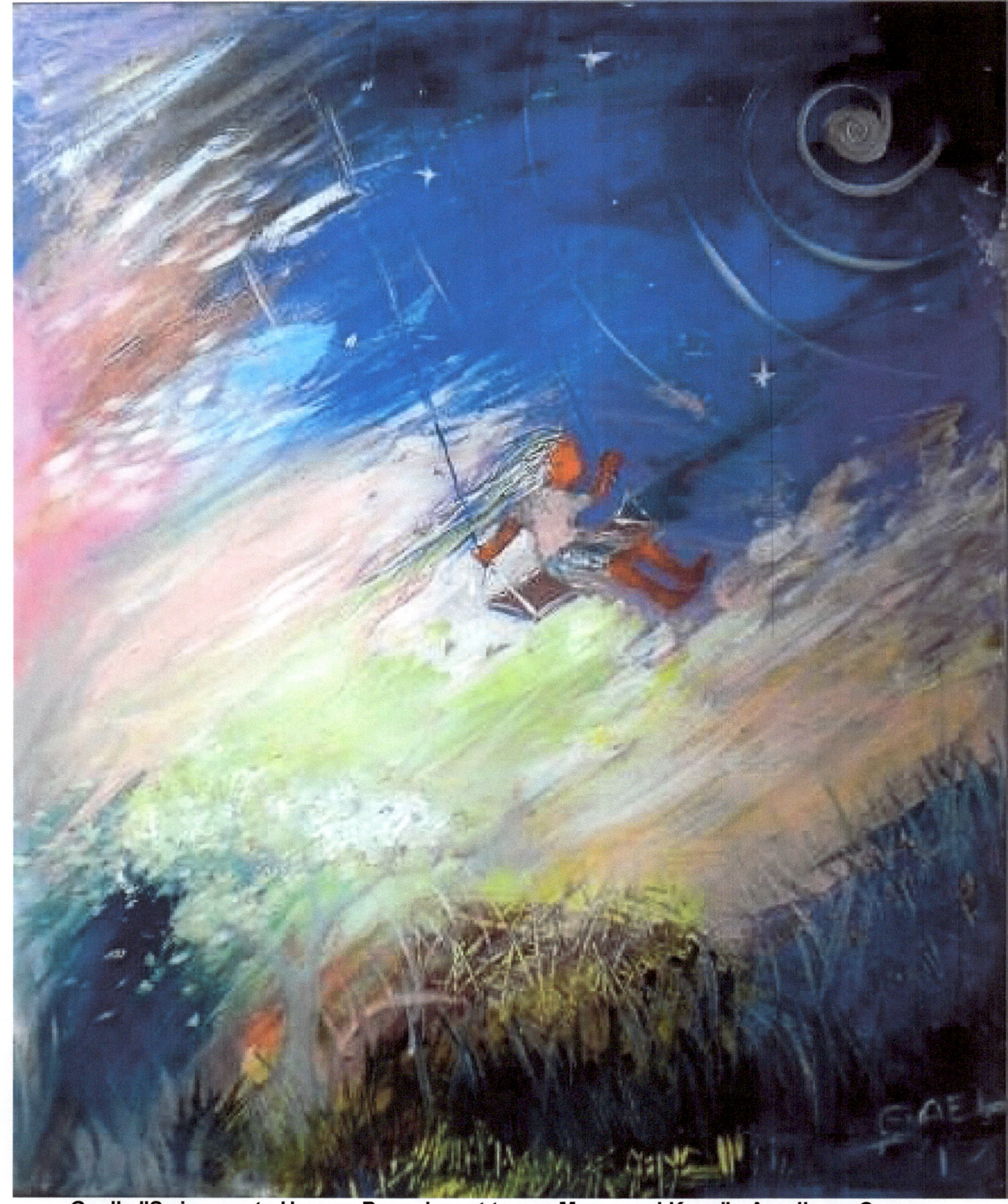

Gael's "Swing me to Heaven Papa, I want to see Mama and Kuya" - Acrylic on Canvas
(for survivors of Haiyan)

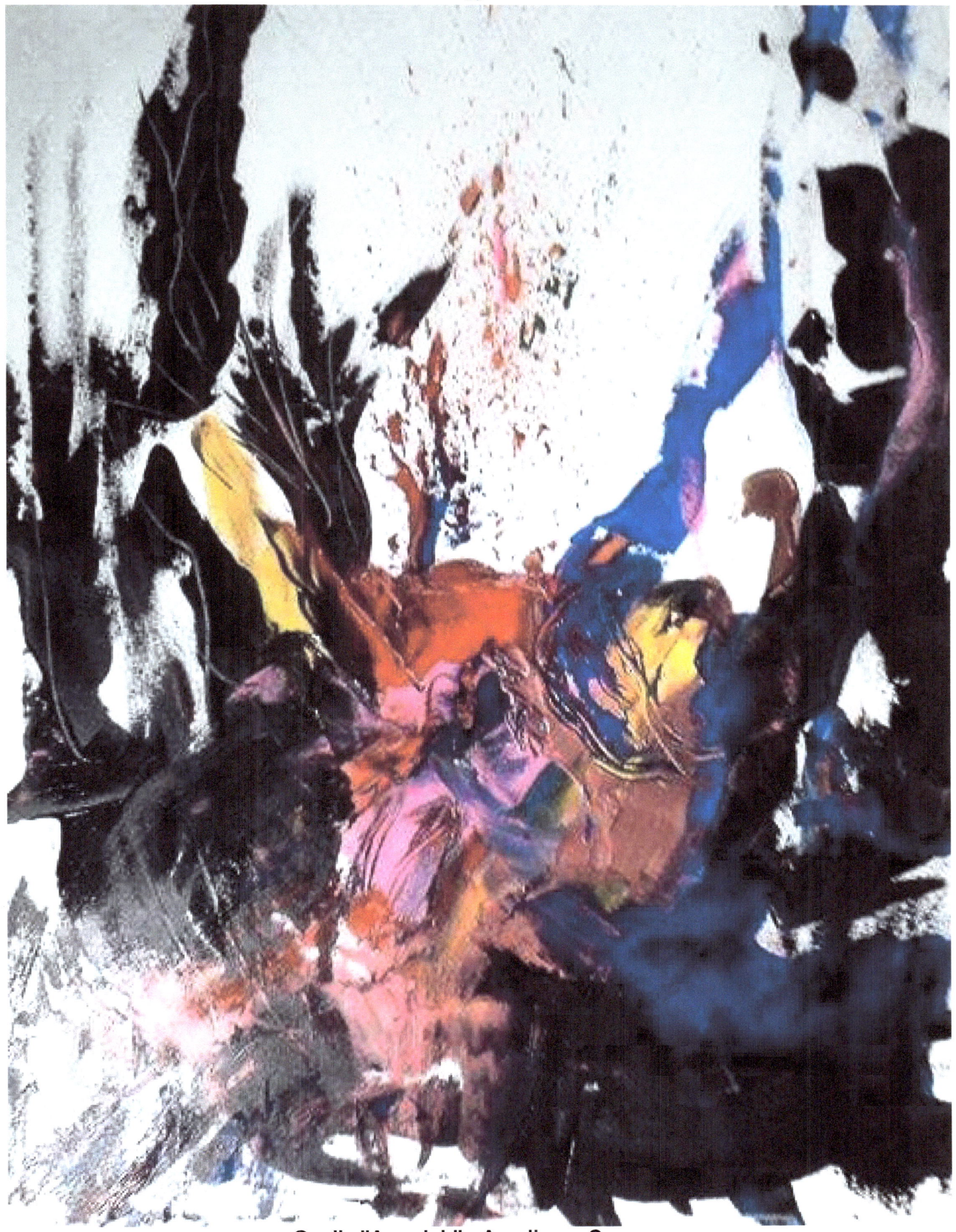

Gael's "Anguish" - Acrylic on Canvas

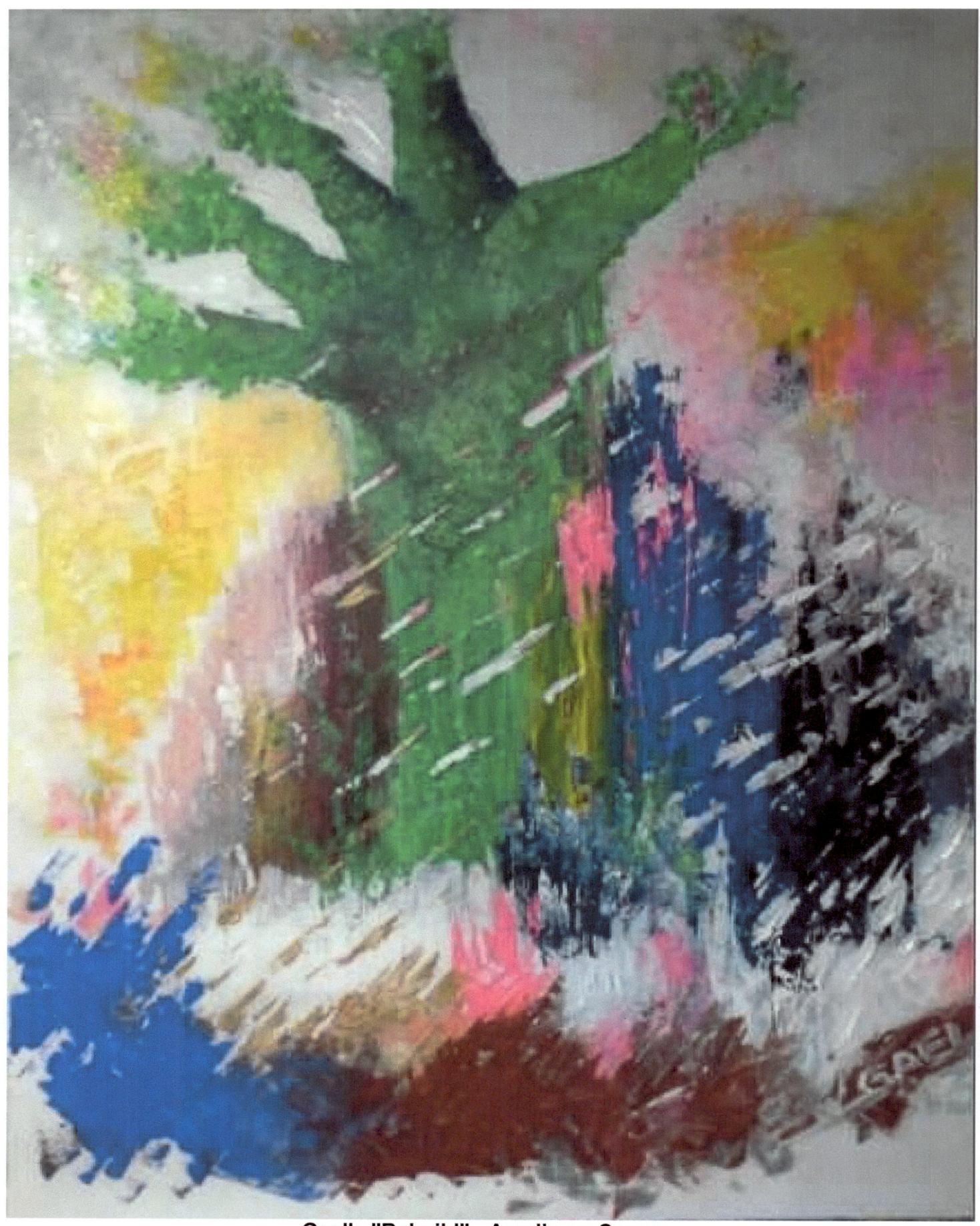

Gael's "Rebuild" - Acrylic on Canvas

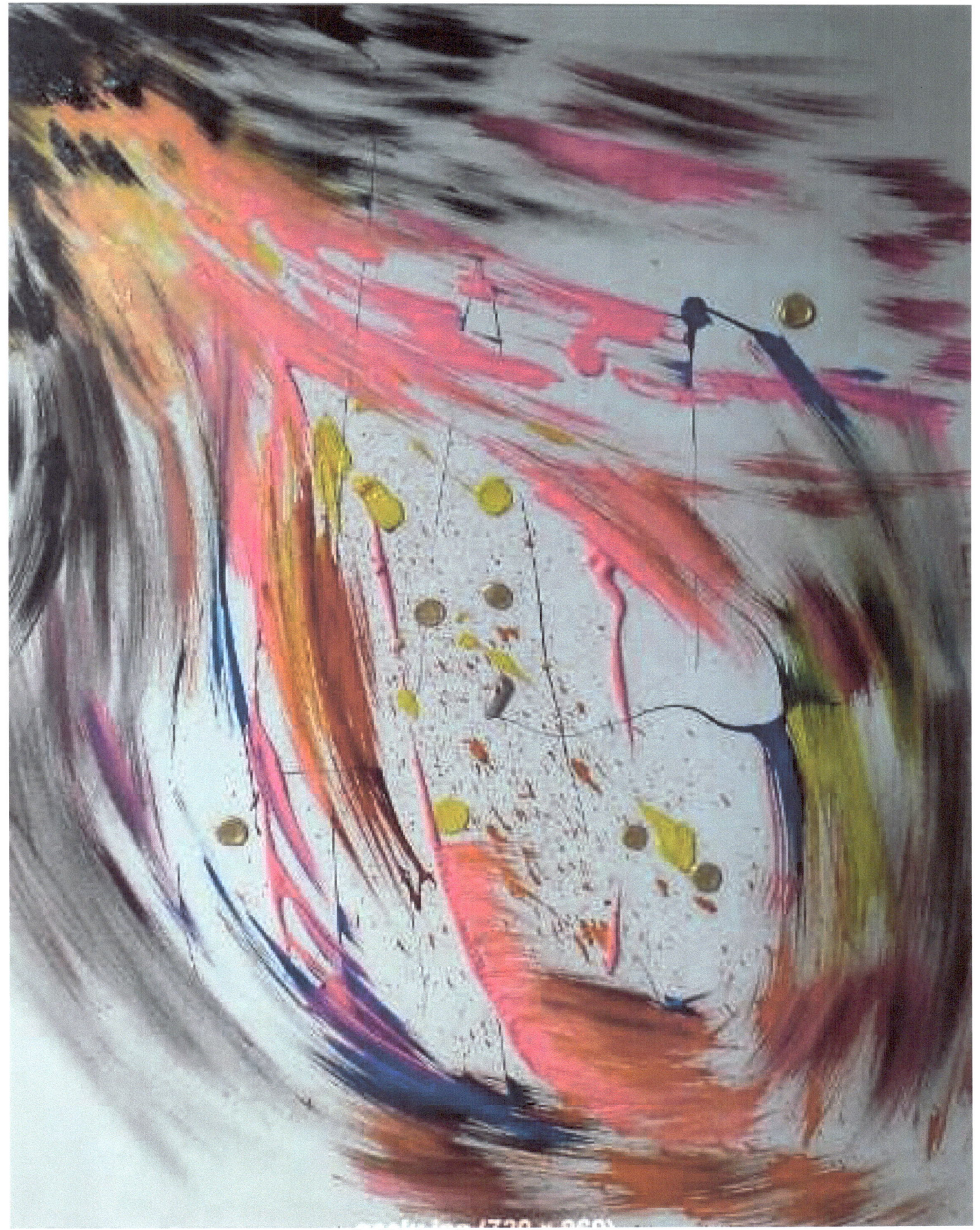

Gael's "Haiyan" - Acrylic on Canvas

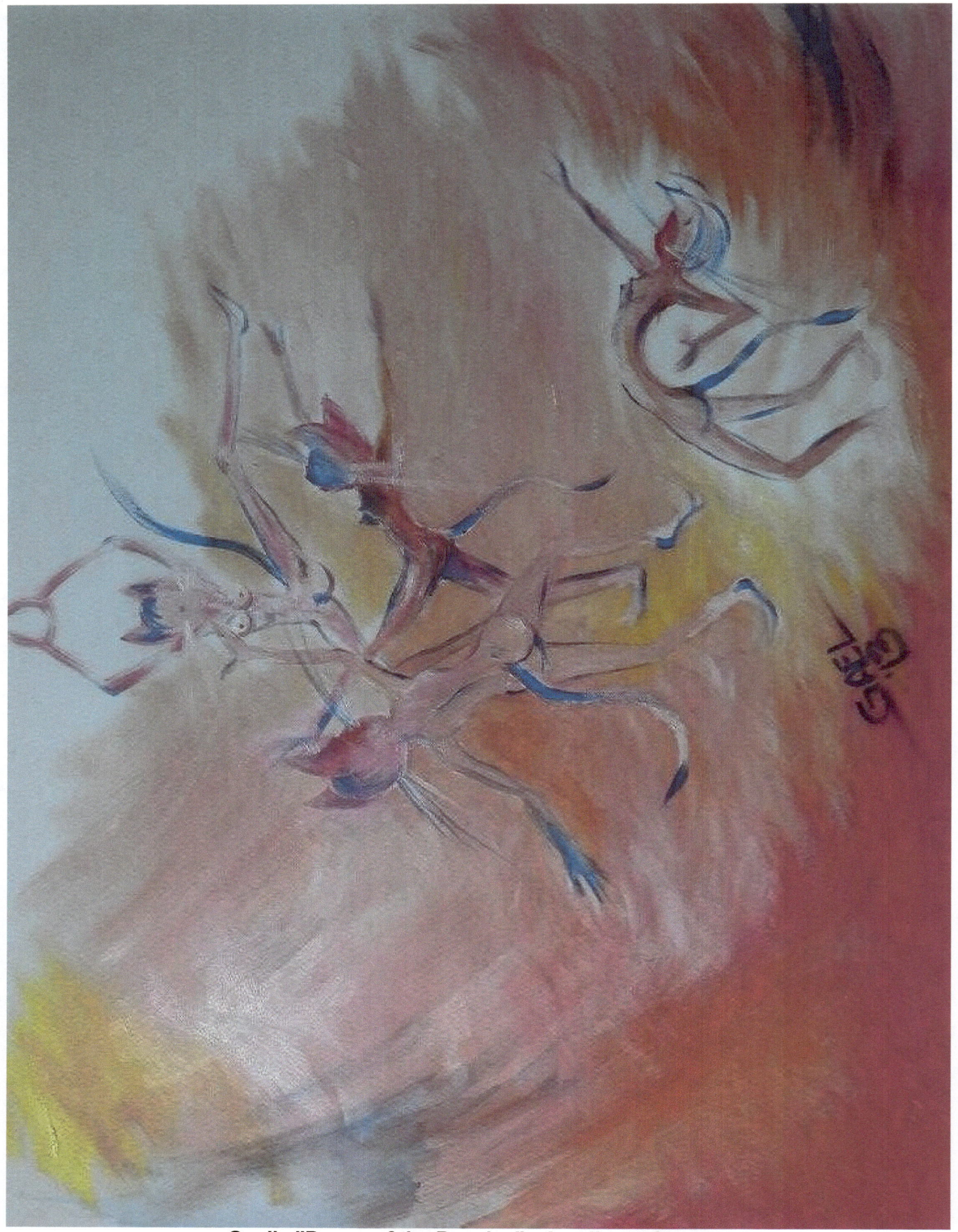

Gael's "Dance of the Pussies" - Acrylic on Canvas

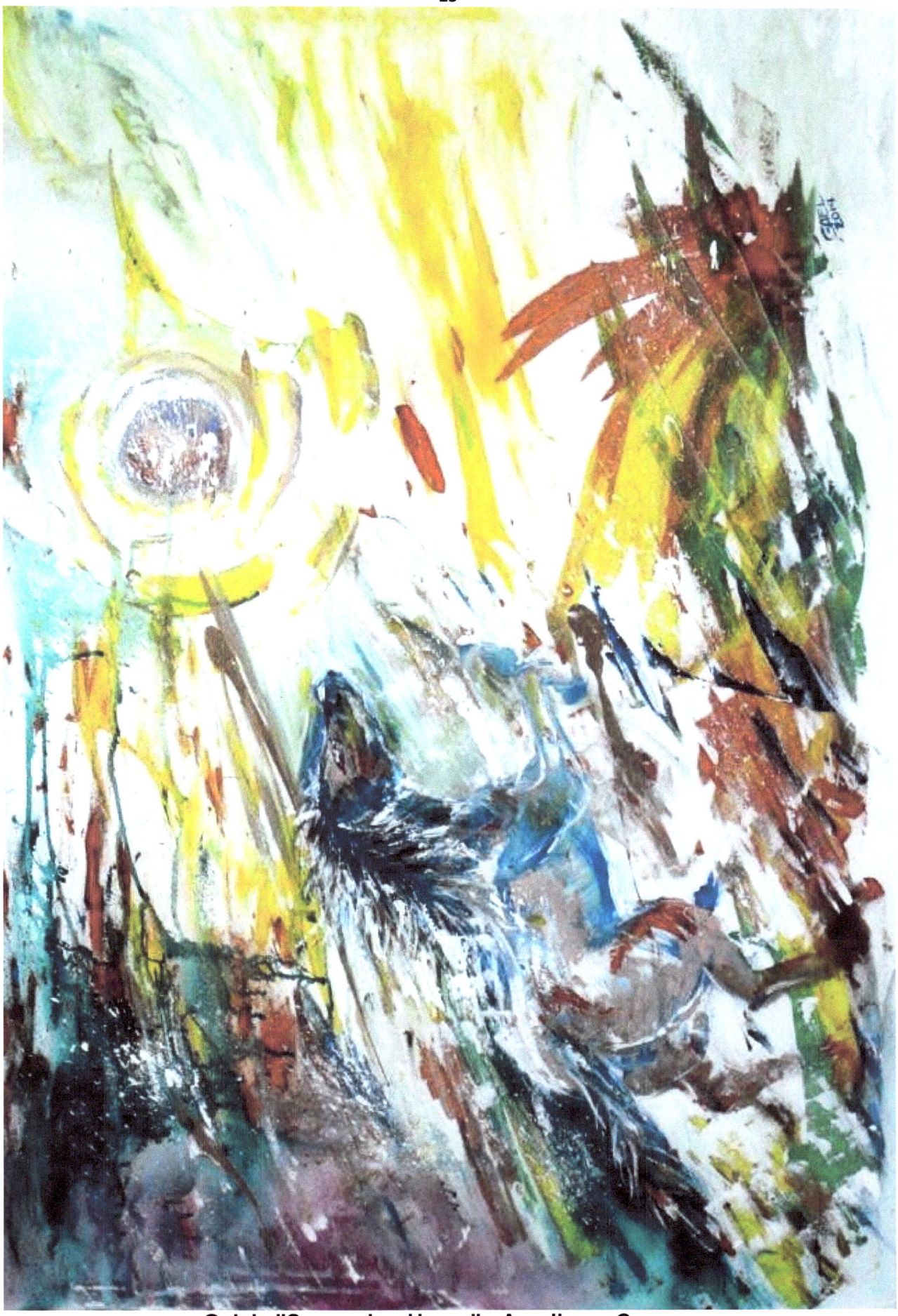

Gale's "Screaming Horse" - Acrylic on Canvas

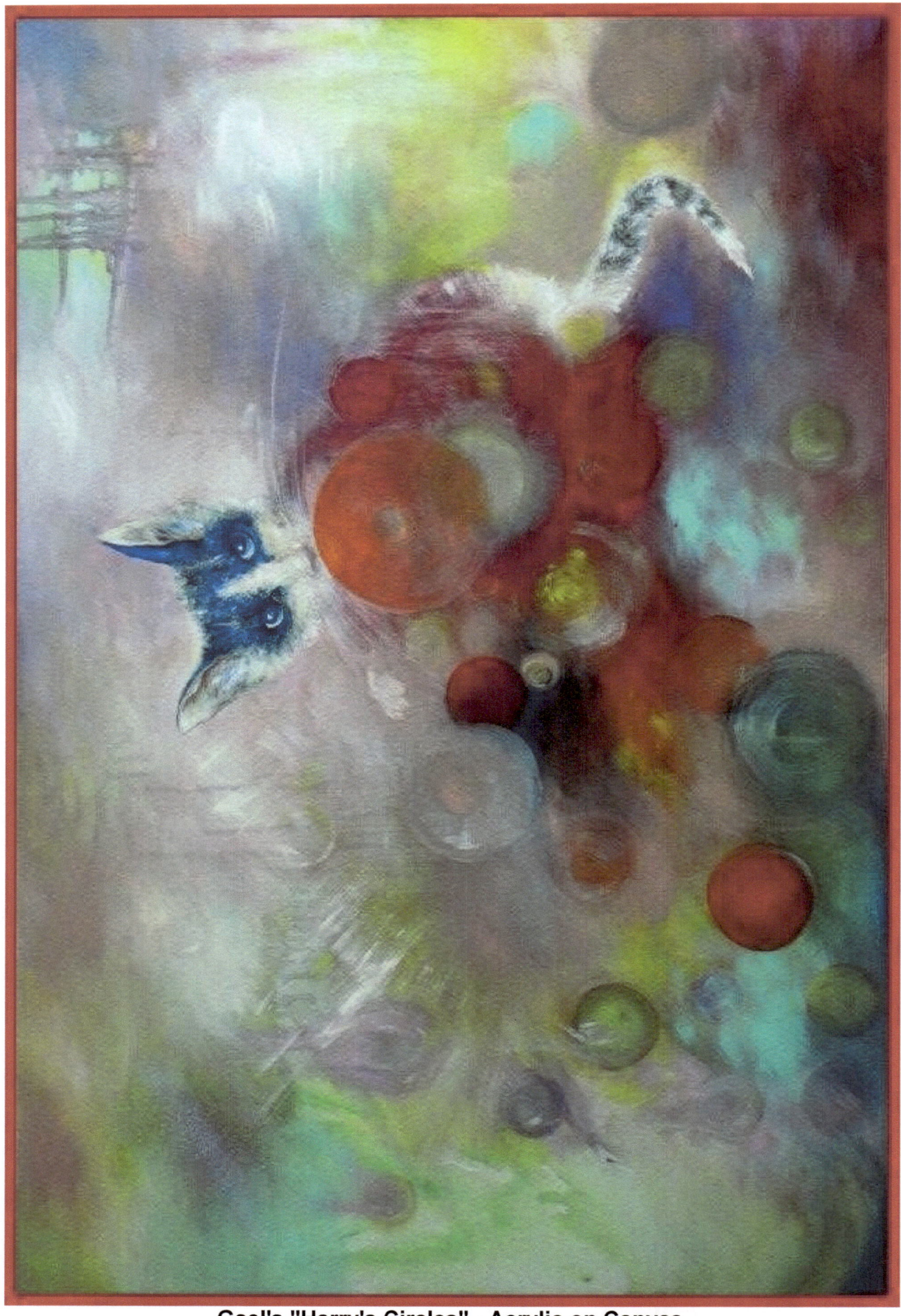

Gael's "Harry's Circles" - Acrylic on Canvas

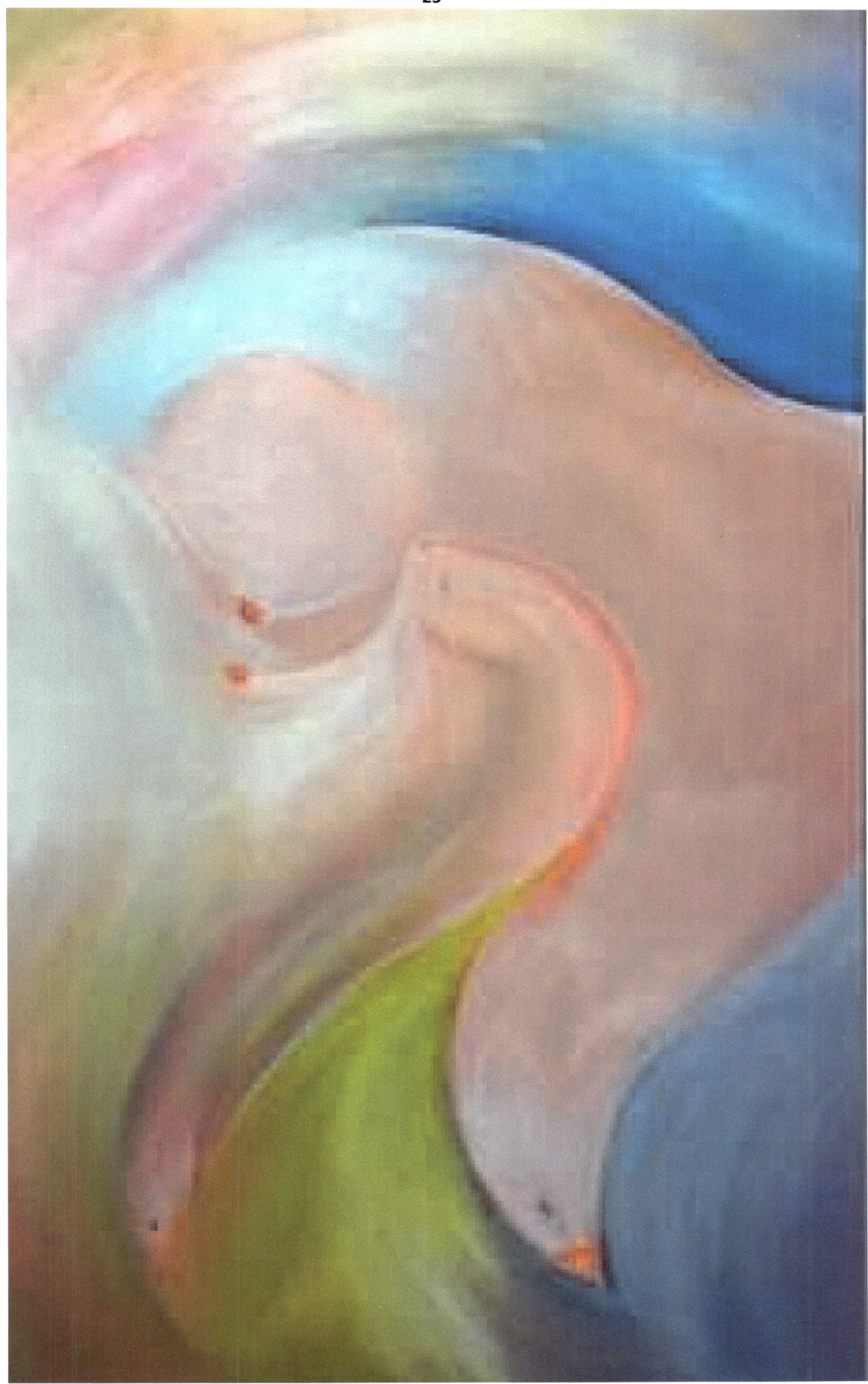

Gael's "Nude Flight" - Acrylic on Canvas

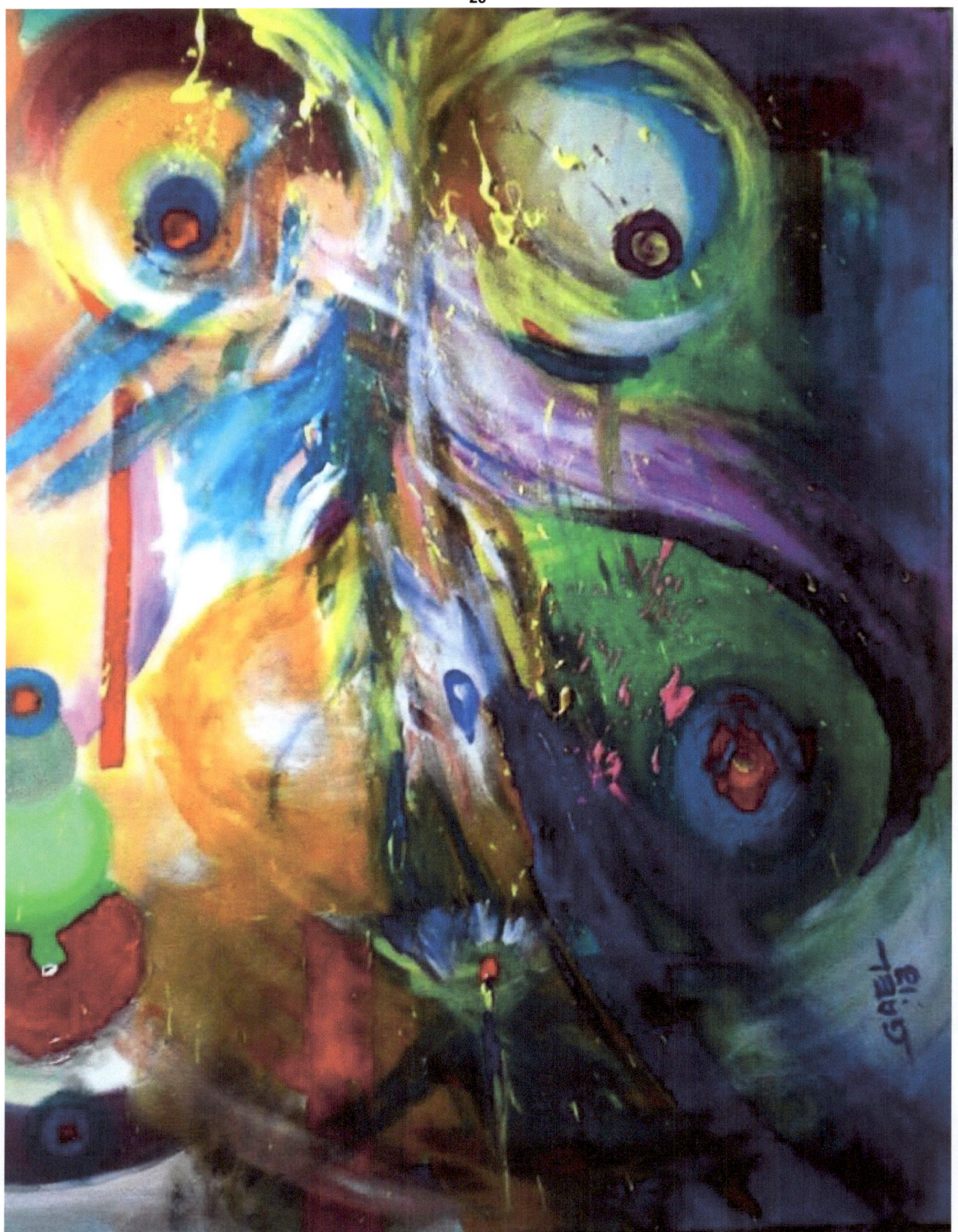

Gael's "Nourishing Circles" - Acrylic on Canvas

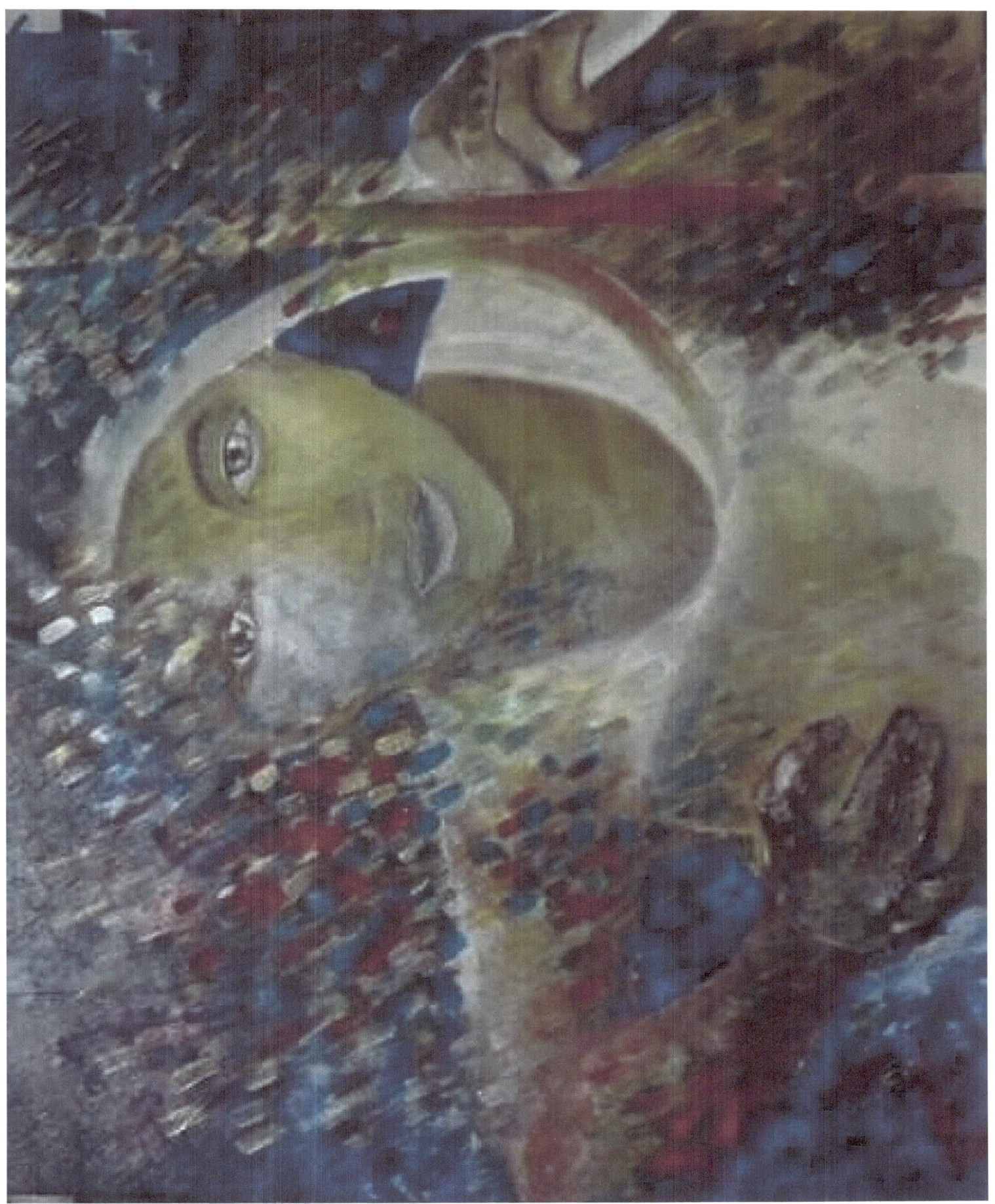

Gael's "The Boy who wanted to Learn" - Acrylic on Canvas

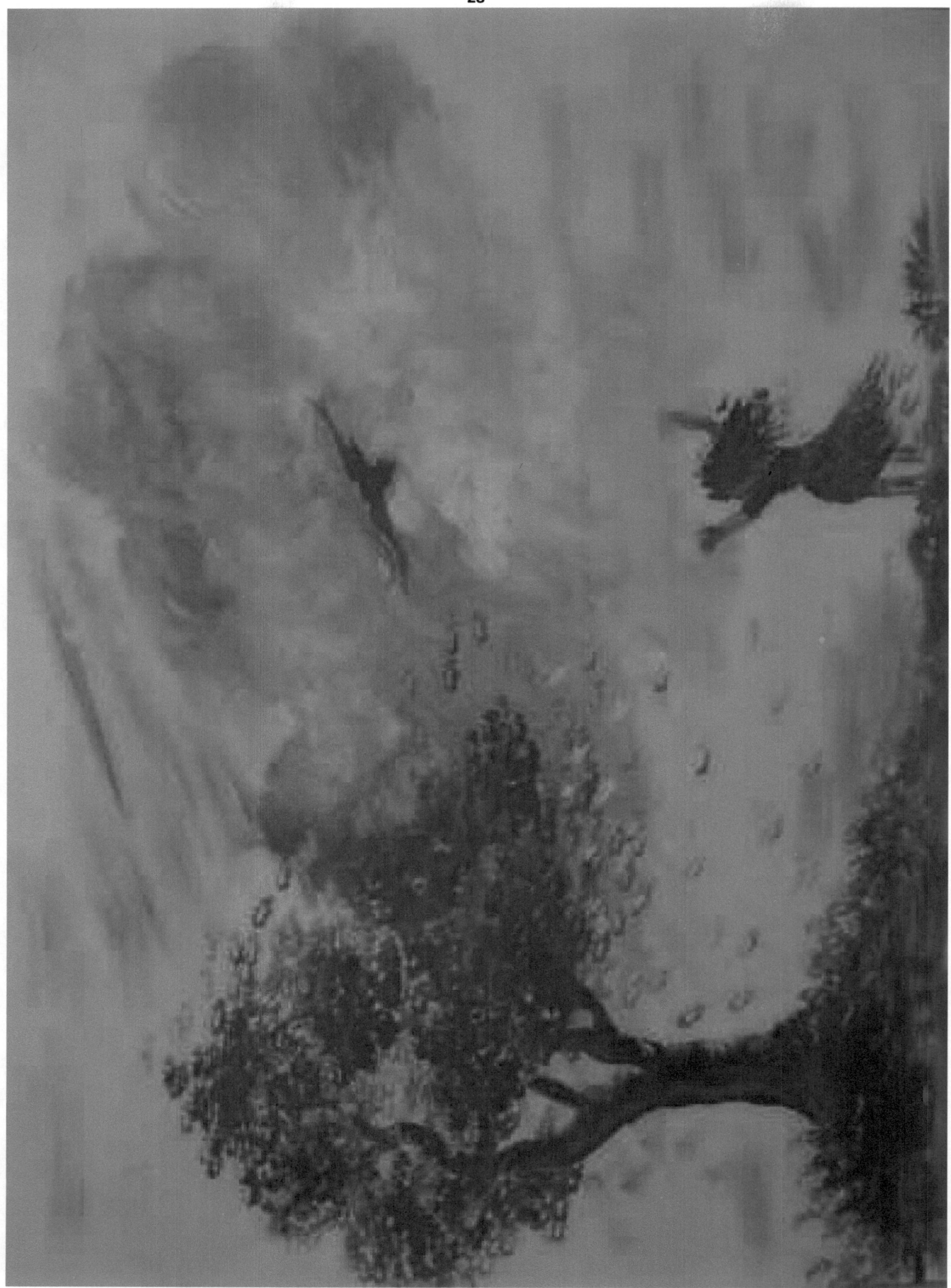

Gael's "The Girl who knew Freedom" - Acrylic on Canvas

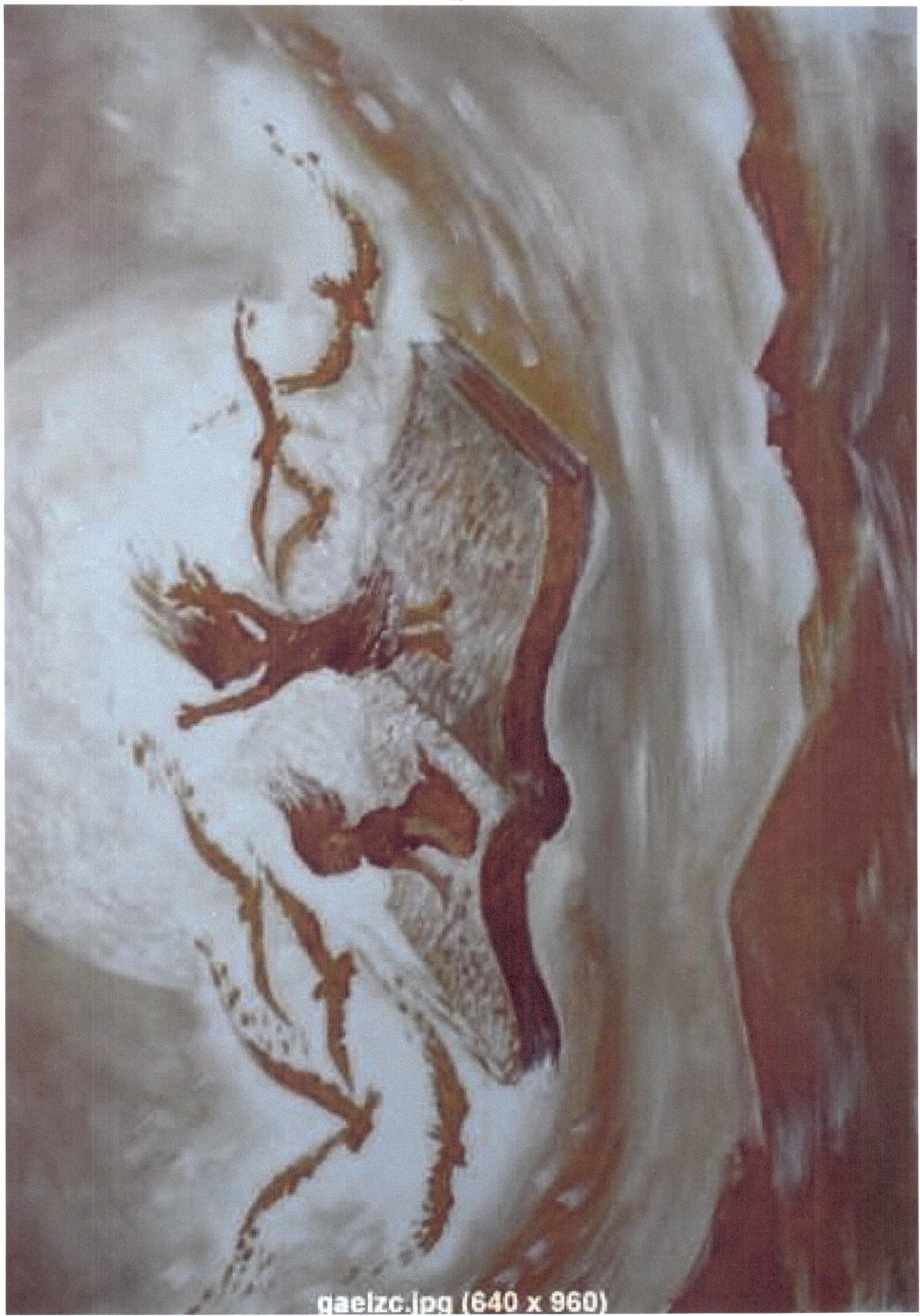

gaelzc.jpg (640 x 960)
Gael's "The Girl who flew on Books" - Acrylic on Canvas

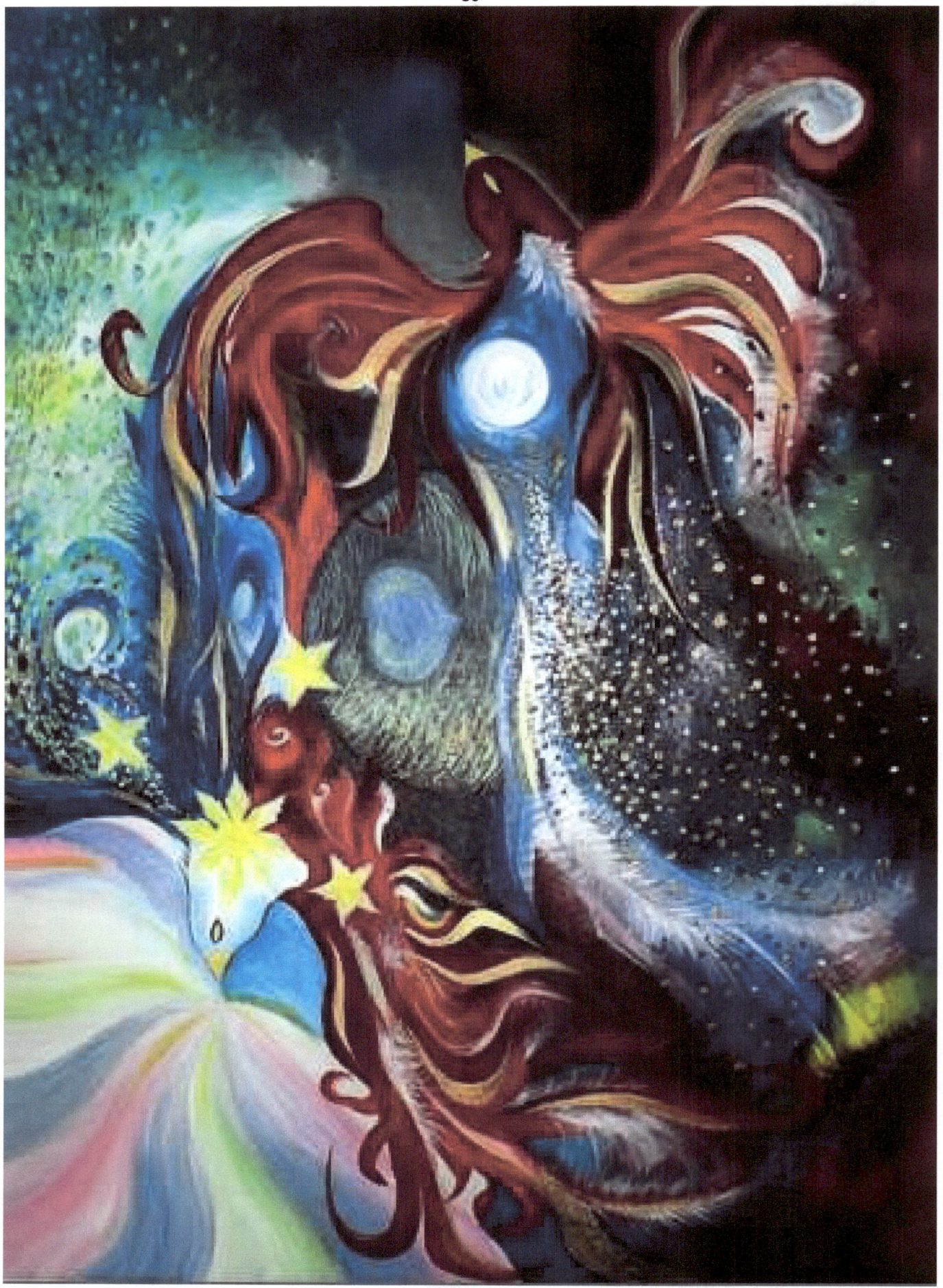

Gael's ". . . ."

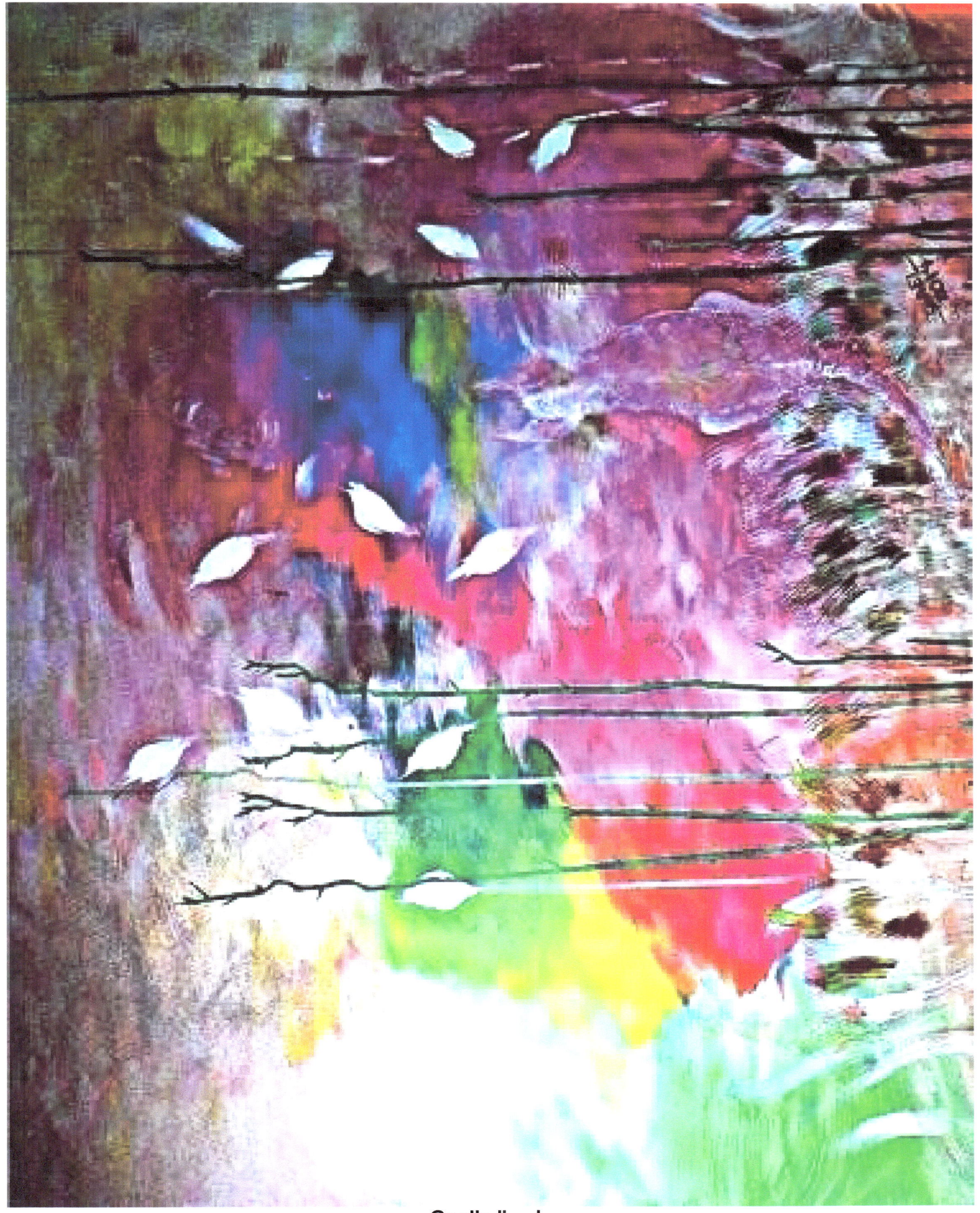

Gael's ". . .'

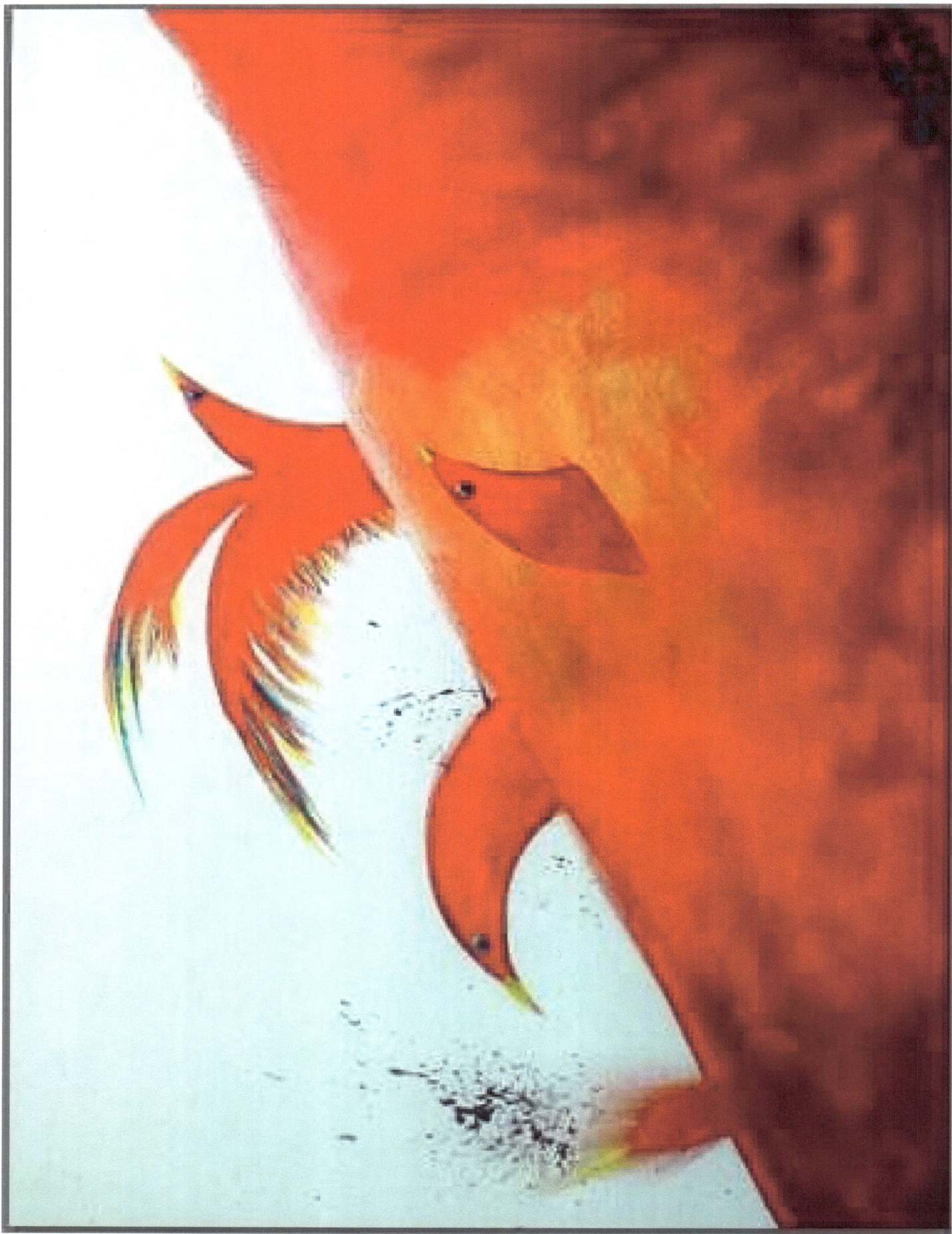

Gael's "......"

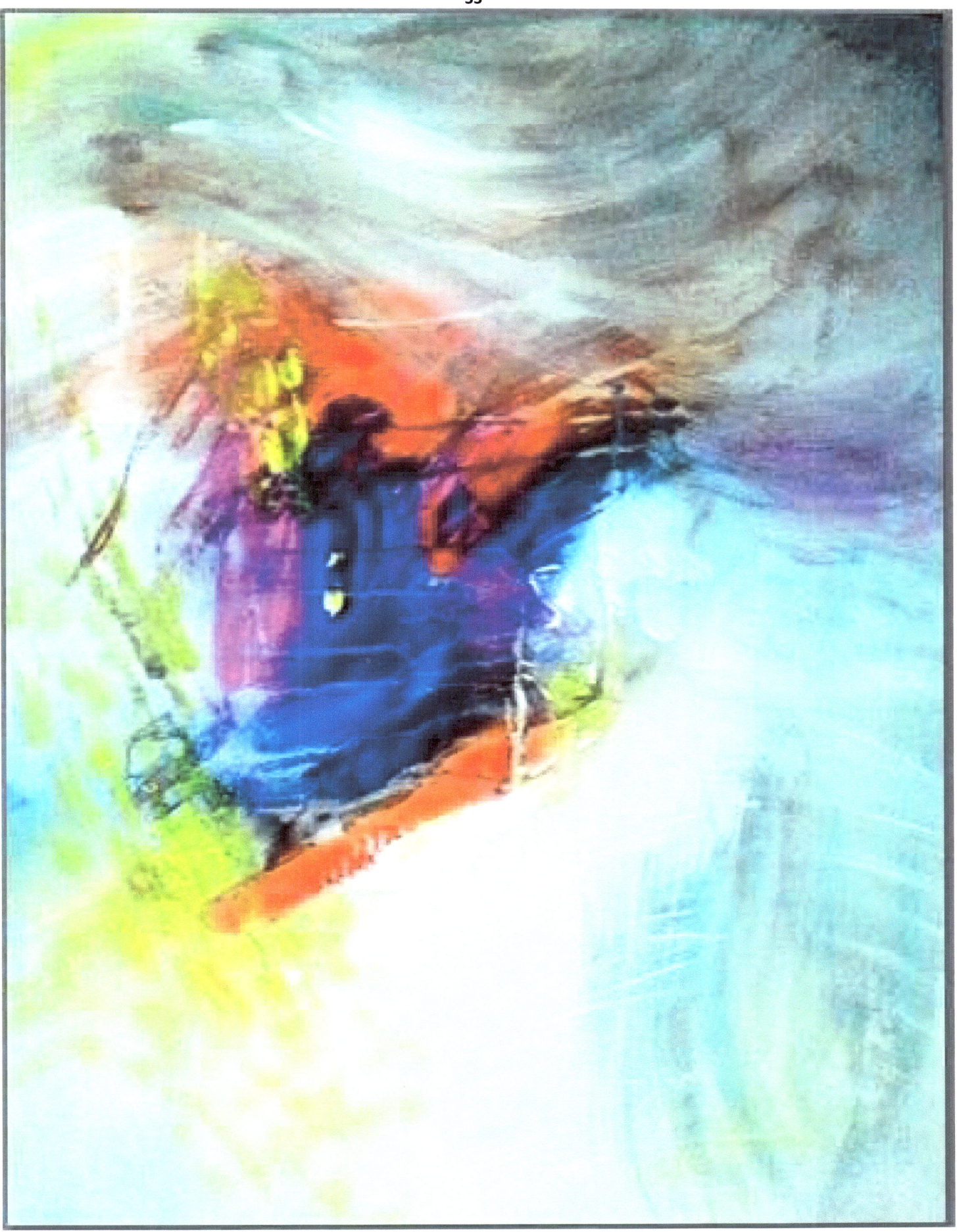

Gael's "....."

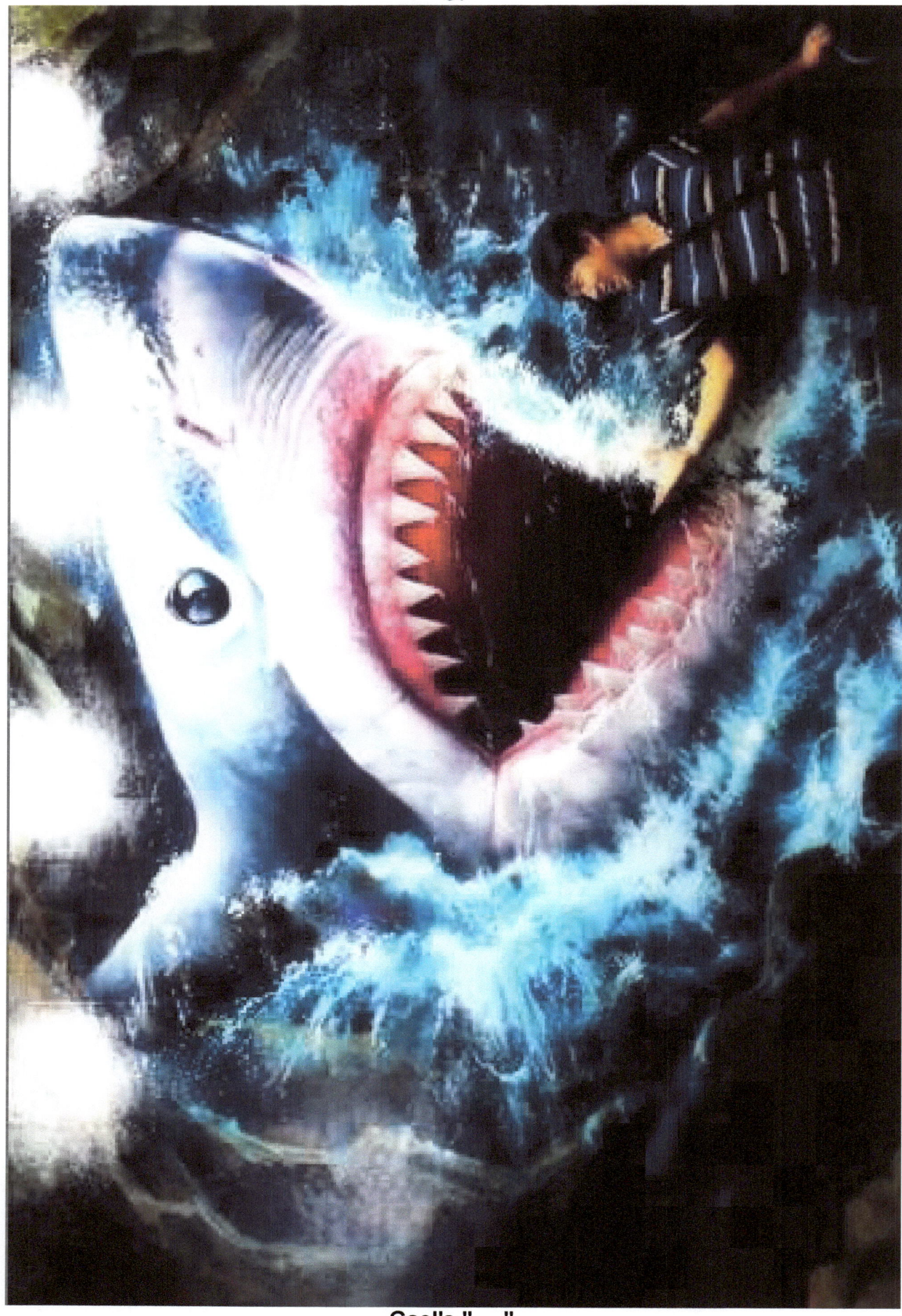

Gael's "....."

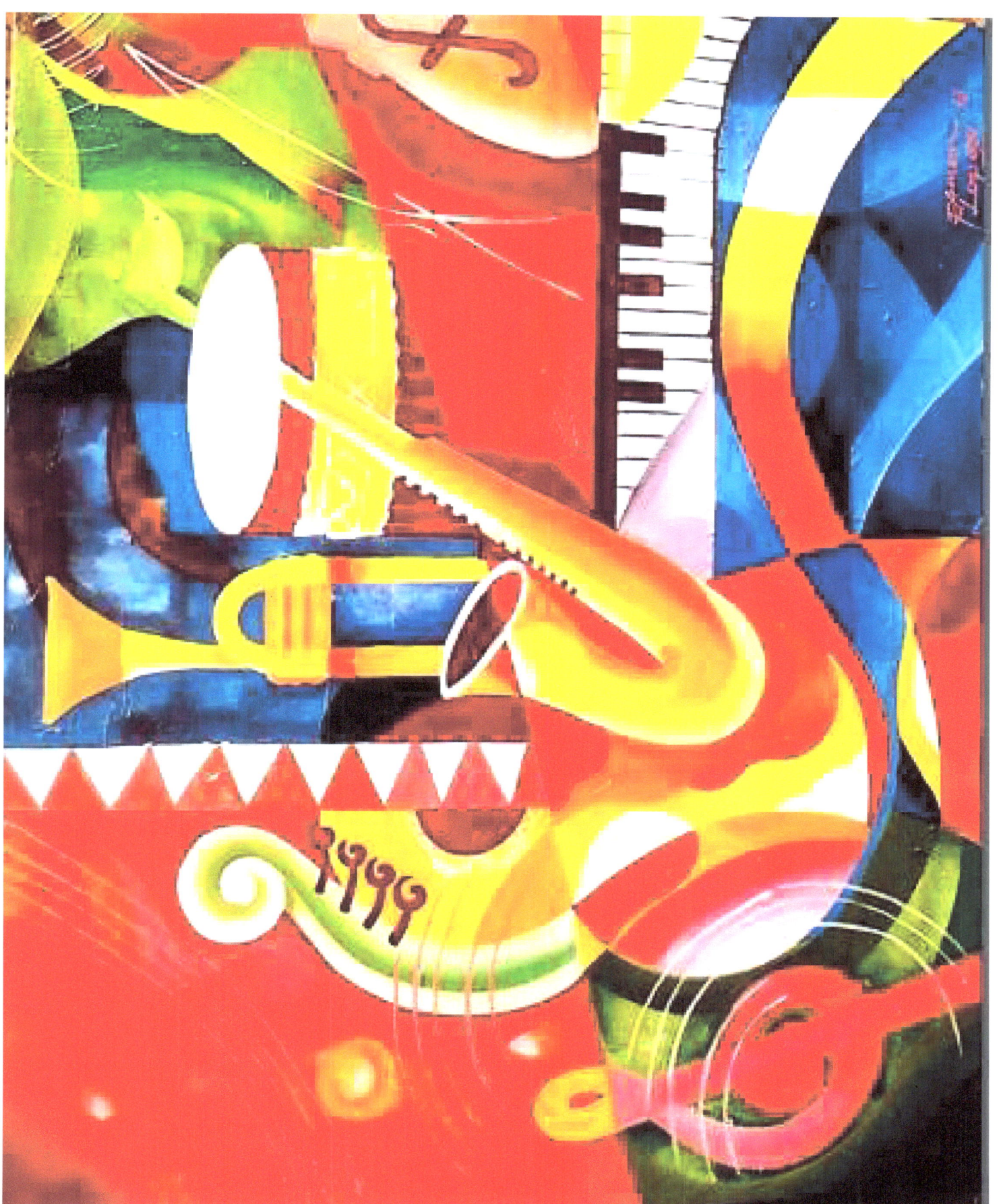

Ramon H. Lopez - The Instruments, 3x4 ft.- Oil, Textured

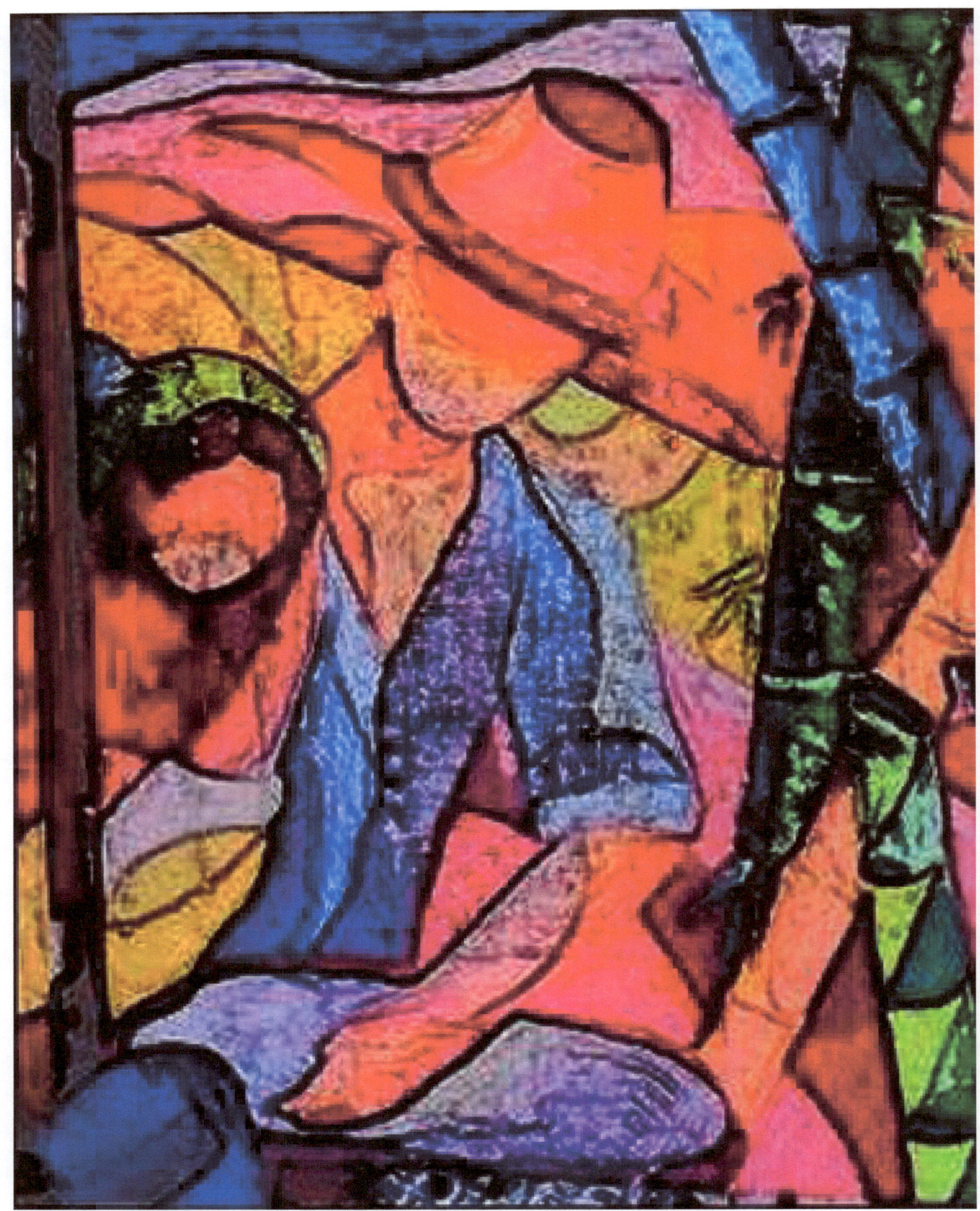

Ramon H. Lopez - Father and Child, 25x30 in.- Oil, Rust, Textured

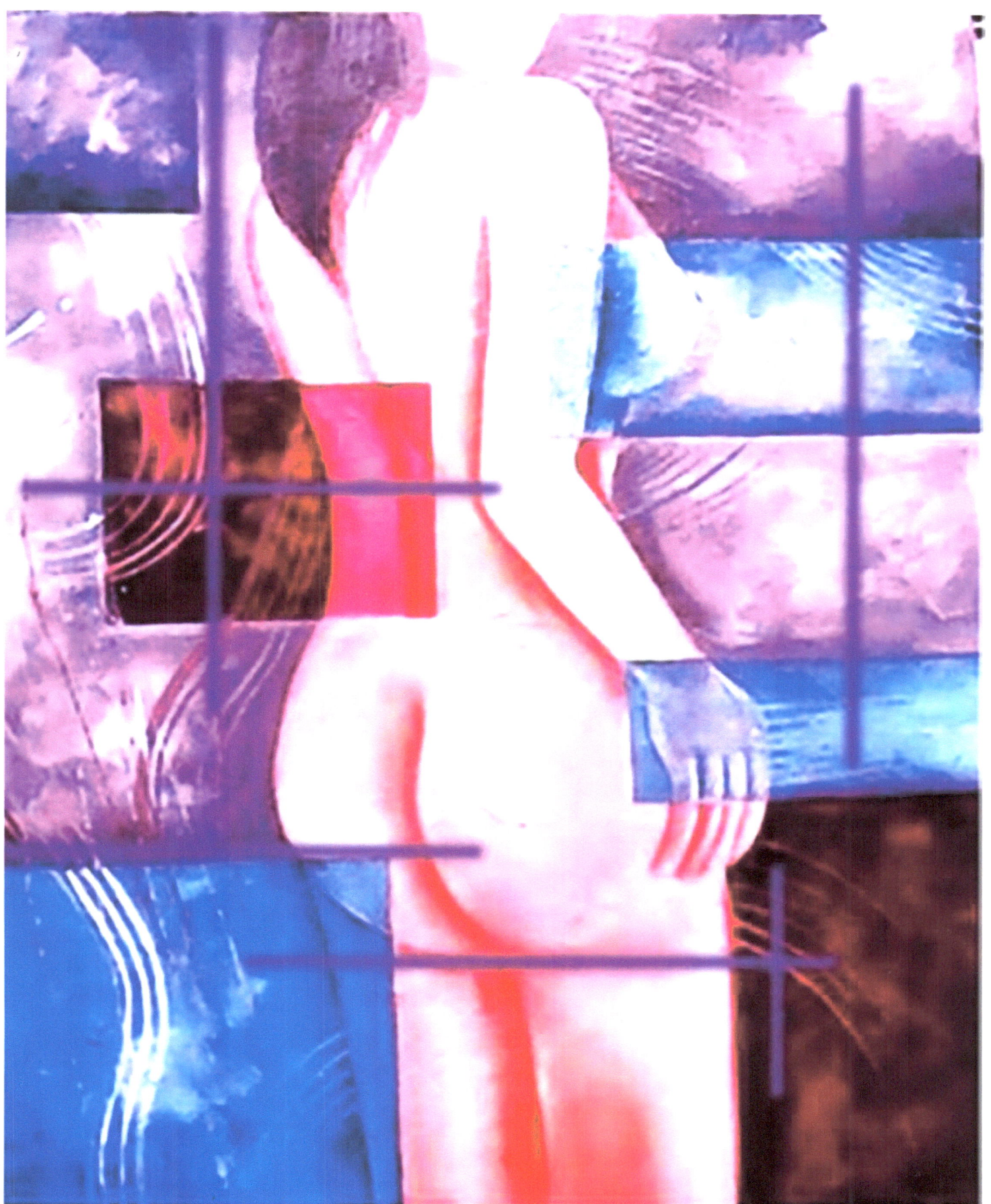

Ramon H. Lopez - Nude Girl, 30x40 in.-Acyrlic, Rust

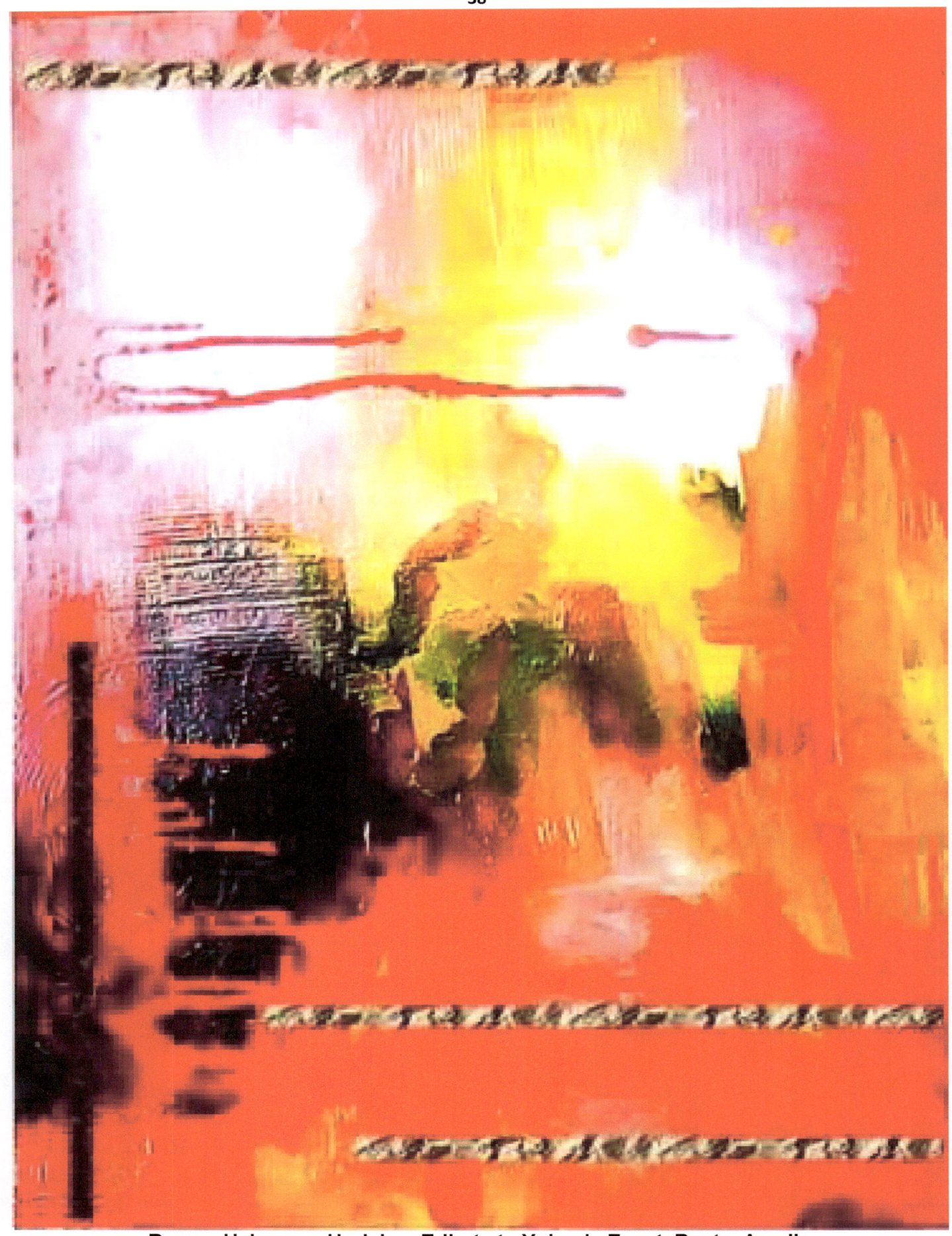

Ramon H. Lopez - Uprising, Tribute to Yolanda Event, Rusty, Acrylic

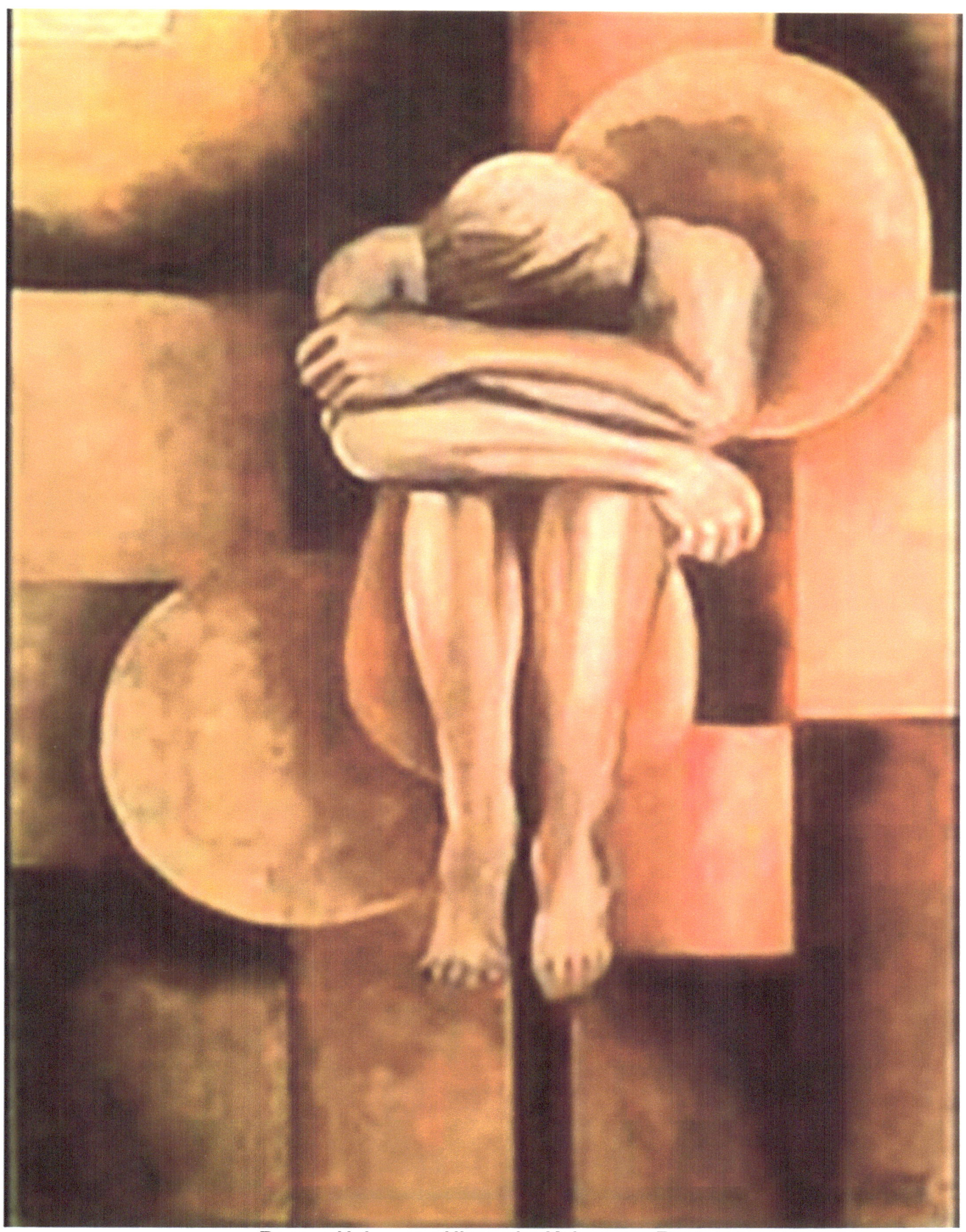

Ramon H. Lopez - Hinagpis, Kalawang, Rust

Publisher's List - Buy online as paperback or kindle, contact
job_elizes@yahoo.com, tatay@usa.com

Writings 1 Book, 2012, Articles by Bambi Harper + Butch Jiimenez + Dr. Phil Stack + Noel Alegre + Toto Causing +_ Melanie Ferrer + Susie Barbieri _ Rodel Ramos + Sylvia Salvador + Tatay Jobo Elizes + + **Writings 2 Book, 2012**, Artices by Gov. Grace Padaca + Melanie Aquino + Toto Causing + Rodel Rodis + Cesar Torres + Joey Concepcion + Charity Guides + Cesar Lumba +_ Casiano Mayor Jr. + Sonny Coloma + Anonymous.+ + **Writings 3A Book, 2012**, Articles by Norman Madrid + Dr. Rene Azurin + Ernie Delfin + Toto Causing + Dr. Jose Abueva + MarVic Cagurangan + Casiano Mayor Jr + Rod Garcia + Roy Gaane + Tatay Jobo Elizes + + **Writings 3B Book, 2012**, Articles by Ceres Busa + John Reyes + Bert Guiang. + + **Writings 4A Book, 2012**, Articles by Dr Jose Abueva + Col. Dennis Acop + Fred Natividad + Irineo P. Goce, KaPule2 + Miguel Reynaldo + Marjorie Ann Elizes Reyes+ + **Writings 4B Book, 2012**, 1. Mi Ultimo Adios (My Last Farewell), *Dr. Jose P. Rizal* + 2. Aling Pagibig Sa Tinubuang Bayan, *Gat. Andres Bonifacio* + Articles by Irineo P. Goce or KaPule2 + + **Writings 5 Book - "Best Hopes" 2010 (About President P-Noy)**, Articles by Tony Meloto + F.SionilJose + Juan L. Mercado + OFWs Letter + Marcelo Tecson + Cesar Torres+ Perry Diaz + Dr. Philip S. Chua + Ernie Delfin + Atty. Ted Laguatan + Frank Wenceslao Jaileen F. Jimeno + Tatay Jobo Elizes + **Writings 6 Book, 2010** + I. SONA - State Of Nation Address - English - *Pres. Benigno Aquino III* + II. SONA - State of Nation Address - Pilipino - *Pres. Benigno Aquino III* + III. First 100 Days peech - Pilipino - *Pres. Benigno Aquino III* + *Artiucles by Bert Guiang* + *Tony Meloto* + *Felicito or Tong C. Payumo* + *Cesar Lumba* + *Flor Lacanilao* + *Juan DelaCruz or Txtmanika* + *Dr. Ramon Marquez* + *Joey Jamito* + *Percival Cruz* + *Rod Garcia* + *Orion Perez Dumdum* + *Sarah Raymundo*. + + **Writings 7 Book, 2010** - My Vintage Pics - Pictorials & Family, Tatay Jobo Elizes + + **Writings 8 Book, 2010**, Articles by Gel Santos Relos + Ms.Mike Portes + Jose Ma. Montelibano + Tony Meloto + Dr. Philip S. Chua + Dr. Cesar D. Candari + Dr. Eliseo Serina + Greg B. Macabenta + Irineo P. Goce or KaPule2 + Percival Cruz + Juan DelaCruz or Textmani + Demosthenes B. Donato. + + **Writings 9 Book, April 2011**, Articles by Judge Simeon dumdum Jr + Gemma Cruz Araneta + Larry Henares Jr + Tony Joaquin + Allen Gaborro + Atty. Toto Causing + Mar-Vic Cagurangn + Emily Espanol Derry, Poet + Elyn Jean Felarca, Poet + Naysan A. Albaytar + Laura Wade, Blogger + Perter Allan Mariano + Marge Trajeco-Aberasturi + Julia Carreon Lagoc + Irineo P. Goce or KaPulle2 + Anonymous. + + **Writings 10 Book, July, 2010**, Articles by Atty.Ted Lagutan + Percival C. Cruz + Allen Gaborro + Peter Allan Mariano + M.L. Munoz + Alvib T. Tabaniag + Resty Odon + Dr. Phili S. Chua + Dr. Cesar D. Candari + Anonymous. + + **Writings 11 Book, August, 2011** + 1, SONA In English and Filipino, by President Benigno Aquino III (P-Noy) + 2, Telltale Signs: SONA and the Dogfight Over Spratlys, by Rodel Rodis + Atty. Ted Laguatan + Tatay Jobo Elizes + Jeremiah M. Opiniano + OFW Journalists + Bob & Carol Hammerslag + Roger P. Olivares + Rob Ceralvo + Anonymous + Irineo P. Goce or KaPule2 + Random. + + **Writings 12 Book, April 2012** + Articles By Orion Perez Dumdum + Julia C. Lagoc + Honorio M. Cruz, MD + Ben Gonzales, MD + Mar-Vic Cagurangan + Marisa Lerias + Gerry Partido + Dr. Cesar D. Candari + Erwin De Leon + Jovelyn B. Revilla + Tatay Jobo Elizes + + **Writings 13 Book, July 2012** + Articles by Raymundo E. Narag + M.L. Munoz + Sonia Barbara gl Munoz + Pamela Joy Agtoto + Percival C. Cruz + Tatay Jobo Elizes + Jhakie Eslit Bayobay + Reygel Saplad Perales.

Timely Writings 14, 2013 + Articles by Cesar F. Lumba + Eugenio Pulmano + Late Jesse Robredo + Antonio Nievera + Alvin T. Tabaniag + Kevin L. Nadal + Anonymous + Fred Natividad + Anonymous + Ellen Tordesillas + Lat Capt. Rene N. Jarque + + **Timeless Writings-15 (TW15), 2014** + Articles by SC Justice Antonio T. Carpio + Atty Dodel Rodis + Atty. Ted Laguatan + Sona by Pres. Benigno Aquino III + F. Sionil Jose + Dr. Philipi Stack + Racz Kelly, Padilla + Bert Armada.

Solo Authored Books: + + +

Book A, **Turning Points**, *Job Elizes Sr,1968 (Reissue 2009)* + + Book B, **Be Considerate For Once**, *Tatay Jobo Elizes (Jr)*, 2013 Book C, **Piglets Unlimited - Wealth**, *Tatay Jobo Elizes, 2009* + + + Book D, **Out of the Misty Sea We Must**, *Cesar Lumba, 2010* + + + Book E, **Fulfilled** – *Gonzales Reynaldo, Editor, 2010* + + + Book F - **Reflections** - *Bert Guiang, 2010* + + + Book G, **Writings 7 - My Vintage Pics**, *Tatay Jobo Elizes, 2010* + Book H, **May Bagwis Ang Pag-ibig**, *Percival C. Cruz* + + + Book I, **Letters To Matrimony**, *Irineo P. Goce, Ka Pule2, 2011* + Book J, **Songs I Wish You Knew**, *Soledad R. Juan, 2010* + + + Book K, **Make My Day**, *Larry Henares Jr., 1993, Re-issue 2011* + Book L, **Our Guerrero Family**, *Tatay Jobo Elizes, 2010* + + + Book M, **Handy Jokes**, *Tatay J. Elizes, 2011* + Book N, **FaveArt 1**, *Tatay Jobo Elizes, 2011* + + Book O, **Beyond idle thoughts**, *MLMunoz, Sept,2011* + + Book P, **Cracks In The Armor**, *Mariano Ngan, Oct 2011* + + + Book Q, **FaveArt 2**, *Tatay Jobo Elizes, 2011* + Book R, **Balitang Kutsero**, *Perry Diaz, Jan 2012* + + + Book S, **FaveArt3**, *Tatay Jobo, 2011* + + Book T, **FaveArt4** ,*2012, Tatay Jobo* + + + Book U, **Stack Family Journals**, *Phil & Fe Stack, 2012* + + + Book V, **Emily, An Adoption Journey**, *Romerl Elizes, 2012* + + + Book W, **Hermes Alegre Art Gallery**, *TJ & Hermes, 2012* + + Book X, **Masaya Din, Malungkot Din**, *Jovelyn B. Revilla, 2012* Book Y, **Tiis, Sipag At Tiyaga**, *Raquel Delfin Padilla, 2012* + + + Book Z, **Until I Meet You**, *Jhackie Eslit Bayobay, 2012* + + + Book AA, **Buhay At Pag-ibig**, *Argel Lucero Tamayo, 2012* + + Book AB, **Hail to the Second Best**, *Dr. Philip Stack, 2012* + + + Book AC, **Life Bus**, *Mommy Joyce Pineda-Faulmino, 2012* + + + Book AD, **My Candid Musings**, *Monette Dioquino Calugay, 2012* + Book AE, **Tickets to Life**, *Maria Lourdes Jesalva, 2012* + + + Book AF, **The Dove Files**, *Mike Portes, 2012* + + + Book AG, **Nursing Vignettes**, *Jocelyn Cerrudo Sese, 2012* + Book AH, **Poor Ba Us**, *R.A. Gubalane, 2012* + + + Book AI, **Summer Idyll**, *Avelina Gil, 2012* + + Book AJ, **Legacy (Pamana)**, *Rachel Astrero, 2012* + + Book AK, **Narratives Old & New**, *Avelina J. Gil, 2013* + + Book AL, **Buhay Saudi**, *Adele J. Esic, 2013* + + Book AM, **Buhay Ofw Atbp**, *Jessica Napat, 2013* + + Book AN, **Mga Tula Ng Buhay**, *Angelita C. Esguerra, 2013* + + Book AO, **Not by Bread Alone**, *Judge Lily V. Magtolis, 2013* + + Book AP, **Jokes Collection-2**, *Tatay Jobo Elizes, 2013* + + + Book AR, **My Writings Sometimes**, *Tatay Jobo Elizes, 2013* + + Book AS, **Sa 'Yo Na Ako**, *Shayne A. Martinez, 2013* + + Book AT, **My Kin's Family Trees**, *Tatay Jobo Elizes, 2013* + Book AU, **Rizal Family Tree & Others**, *Tatay Jobo Elizes, 2013* + + Book AV, **Make My Day-2, Nice & Nasty**, *L. Henares, 2013 (1993)* + + Book AW, **Make My Day-3, Cecilia, Love**, *L.Henares, 2013 (1993)*Book AX, **Handy Lyrics-1**, *Tatay Jobo Elizes, 2013* + + Book AY, **Ang Biblos**, *Rev. Dr. Eugenio Guerrero, 2014 (1929)* + + Book AZ, **Make My Day-4, Sweet & Sour**, *L. Henares, 2014 (1993)* + + Book BA, **Life's Journey, True Stories**, *Dr. Phil Stack, 2014* + + Book BB, **Gerry Gil Writings**, *Danny Gil* + + Book BC, **Mr. President**, *Hermie Rotea, 2014* + + Book BD, **Nostalgic Pics 1**, *Tatay Jobo Elizes, 2014* + + Book BE, **MakeMyDay-5, Saints & Sinners**, *Henares, 2014 (1993)* + + Book BF, **MakeMyDay-6, Villains & Heroes**, *Henares, 2014 (1993)* + + Book BG, **Nostalgic Pics 2 (ElizesClan)**, *TatayJE, 2014* + + Book BH, **MakeMyDay-7, Tough & Tender**, *Henares, 2014(1993)* + + Book BI, **MakeMyDay-8, Light & Shadow**, *Henares, 2014(1993)* + + Book BJ, **MakeMyDay-9, Give & Take**, *Henares, 2014(1993)* + + Book BK, **MakeMyDay-10, ToBeOrNotToBe**, *Henares, 2014(1993)* + Book BL,**Emily Forever In Love**, Poems,*Emily Espanol Derry, 2013* + + Book BM, **The Sinatra Songbook**, *Henares, 2014* + + Book BN, **The Gaborro Reader**, *Allen Gaborro, 2010*

Self-Publisher
Tatay Jobo Elizes was born in Manila, Philippines, in 1934, retiree, now based in NY, busy publishing as a hobby.

Acknowledgement & Dedication
Gratitude and acknowledgment belongs to all those who support my hobby and encourage me to continue publishing books. **I heartily dedicate this** to my wife, **Cora**, my children, **Tetchie, Chevy & Abeth, and Marie & Bimbo**, my grandchildren, **Karines & Aung, Noelle, Chad, Marjo, Jeb, Marvin & Marty**, great-grandsons **Jason Win & Carson** and my siblings **Susan, Hilda, Bobby, Bey & Manny** and to all my extended relatives.

ISBN
Printed in the United States of America under ISBN code below.
ISBN-13-978: 978-1500236861 + + + ISBN-10: 1500236861
Publisher's Contact: job_elizes@yahoo.com, tatay@usa.com
My websites: http://tinyurl.com/mj76ccq + + + www.jobelizes.com
"Buy A Book or Gift for Somebody - paperback or kindle edition online"

www.ingramcontent.com/pod-product-compliance
Lightning Source LLC
Chambersburg PA
CBHW050357180526

45159CB00005B/2048